JANUARY–APRIL 1997

VOLUME 13 / PART 1

Edited by **Grace Emmerson and John Parr**

The Bible Reading Fellowship
OPENING THE BIBLE

Writers in this issue

Selected Psalms **Gareth Watts** was a minister with the Welsh Congregational Churches at Llanberis and Barry and lectured at the University School of Theology at Cardiff before moving to Aberystwyth in 1992 as Professor of Biblical Studies at the Lampeter–Aberystwyth School of Theology and the College of Welsh Independents. He has written a Welsh language commentary on Joel and Amos.

Acts **E. Margaret Embry** was for many years a tutor/lecturer in New Testament Studies at Trinity College, Bristol. She is now retired, but continuing ministry in South Bristol.

Genesis **David Reimer** is a tutorial fellow in Hebrew and Old Testament at Regent's Park College, Oxford. He is also active in lay preaching among the Baptist churches. His published work includes a book on Jeremiah, and his current research interests lie in the area of Old Testament theology.

Matthew (3) **John Parr** is Priest in Charge of Harston and Hauxton near Cambridge, and Director of Continuing Ministerial Education in the Ely Diocese. He is joint-editor of *Guidelines*.

Revelation **John Sweet** retired in 1994 as Dean of Selwyn College, Cambridge and University lecturer in New Testament Studies. He has published a major commentary on Revelation.

Hosea **Alec Gilmore**, a Baptist minister, was formerly editor of Lutterworth Press and Director of Feed the Minds. He lectures in the Old Testament in the Universities of Brighton and Sussex. His published work includes *Agenda for Development*, on the literature needs of the developing world.

Editors' Letter

Another new year—we send our best wishes to all *Guidelines* readers throughout the world. As the year unfolds, we pray that in our many and varied circumstances, faith may grow and prayer be enriched through our common study of the word of God. We hope too that new members may be added to this Bible Reading Fellowship over the year. If you are a new reader, why not write to us and let us know what you think about *Guidelines*?

We begin the year with readings of selected Psalms by Professor Gareth Watts, who is already known to some readers. His selection includes not only Psalms with which we can readily identify, but also several of the most difficult 'imprecatory Psalms'. In these, the Psalmist calls on God to pour out his wrath on his enemies. Many Christians find such sentiments alien to their belief, and as a result the imprecatory Psalms are often ignored. Professor Watts faces the question as to whether there can be any justification for reading these ancient songs in today's world.

From there we move to one of the best-loved parts of the New Testament, the Acts of the Apostles. Its racy narrative of the birth and early extension of the Church is well served by Margaret Embry's notes on chapters 1–12. David Reimer is a new writer to *Guidelines*. He brings fresh insights to the familiar opening chapters of Genesis. Two weeks into Lent we enter the passion narrative in Matthew's Gospel. The readings from Matthew 21–28 take us through the last week of Jesus' ministry in Jerusalem. During Holy Week we are able to concentrate on the last hour of Jesus' earthly life, before entering into Matthew's appreciation of the joy of Easter.

After Easter we are caught up into the visions of the risen Christ conveyed by the last book of the Bible, Revelation. John Sweet has devoted much of his life to studying this work, whose imagery can be both uplifting and puzzling. His notes deal with some of the awkward questions raised by one of the most mysterious and fascinating parts of the Bible. The issue ends with something more down to earth, the book of Hosea. Alec Gilmore's sensitive approach views the prophet in the light of some of the problems of contemporary society.

We hope that you enjoy the material in this issue. It will certainly make you think—we trust that it will also nourish your prayer and encourage you as you walk in the way of our Lord Jesus Christ.

Grace Emmerson, John Parr
Editors

The BRF Prayer

O God our Father,
in the holy scriptures
you have given us your word
to be our teacher and guide:
help us and all the members of our Fellowship
to seek in our reading
the guidance of the Holy Spirit
that we may learn more of you
and of your will for us,
and so grow in likeness to your Son,
Jesus Christ our Lord.

THE BRF
Magazine

A Message from Her Majesty Queen Elizabeth The Queen Mother

CLARENCE HOUSE
S.W.1

As Patron I am so pleased that the seventy-fifth anniversary of the Bible Reading Fellowship is to be celebrated in Westminster Abbey on 30th January 1997. This underlines the fact that for the greater part of a century a society has existed to encourage people to read the Bible.

Familiarity with the knowledge imparted by the Bible is the receipt for leading a life of rectitude in accordance with the word of God. It is worth noting that many of the evils which beset us today would be avoided by strict adherence to the precepts of the ten commandments. In the New Testament can be found the words of Christ which contain the essential teaching for leading a spiritual life.

In happier days when everyone went to Church and children attended Sunday School these precepts became part of everyday life. Now, it is largely through the work of the Bible Reading Fellowship that people are led to follow the path which will lead them to fuller life in this world and the hope of eternal felicity.

ELIZABETH R
Queen Mother

January 1997

Richard Fisher writes

Happy New Year! On behalf of all of us at BRF may I offer you our warmest greetings and best wishes for this new year. 1997 is a very special year for BRF as we celebrate our 75th Anniversary, and we are particularly delighted to be able to include in this issue of the *Magazine* a special Message from Her Majesty Queen Elizabeth The Queen Mother, who has been Patron of the Fellowship since 1952.

BRF has come a long way since the first leaflet of Bible readings was produced by The Revd. Leslie Mannering for his congregation in January 1922. We hope that you will share with us in celebrating and giving thanks to God for all he has done over the years in and through BRF, its trustees, staff, authors and of course the hundreds of thousands of men, women and children throughout the world who have been helped by its Bible reading notes and books.

You can play your part!

Many readers have approached us to ask what they can do to help promote BRF and its ministry during this anniversary year. The answer is very simple! If you think that the Bible is important, that it is relevant to Christians in 1997, that through it God still speaks to us today, and if you yourself are a regular Bible reader (and the very fact that you're reading this publication suggests that the answer to all these questions is 'Yes!'), then please join us in encouraging others to read it for themselves. Without doubt the most effective means of encouraging others is through personal recommendation.

Why not tell a friend, colleague, neighbour, family member why you read the Bible, how you read it, the resources that you use. You never know, you might get them started on a habit of a lifetime!

Disciple

By the time you read this you may already have heard about *Disciple—Becoming Disciples through Bible Study*, an exciting new initiative which is now available in the UK through a partnership between The Foundery Press and BRF. You will find more details about *Disciple* on page 12.

Large Print New Daylight

It was with regret that we had to increase the price of the large print version of *New Daylight* in September last year. As it became evident that we could no longer sustain the level of subsidy required, the choice that faced us was either to increase the cover price and so reduce the amount of subsidy needed, or discontinue the publication and thus deprive nearly 2,000 subscribers of their daily notes. The decision seemed obvious to us, and in fact the price increase (of £1 per copy, effective September 1996) was the first since the large print version first became available in September 1992.

Special Projects News

Last year we sent some books to ministers in Papua New Guinea and were overwhelmed and humbled by the letters of thanks and appreciation which we received from them. It made us realize afresh just how much we take the availability of books and resources for granted.

We hope to be able to do more to equip those in ministry in situations where either books are unavailable or in short supply, or where funds for obtaining them are limited. The response from those subscribers with whom we shared this idea last year was very encouraging. The funds donated for this purpose have enabled us to send more books to the ministers in Papua New Guinea, and to give further quantities of BRF books and notes for use in ministry among prisons in the UK. It is our hope that during this anniversary year we will be able to expand this work even further, so that ministers and pastors may be better equipped for their biblical teaching and preaching ministry.

Lent

For many years now BRF has published a new book(s) each Lent. All of these follow the pattern of a Bible passage (printed in full), comment and prayer for every day from Ash Wednesday to Easter Sunday. Most contain questions for group discussion as well. Extracts from both new books for Lent 1997 are included in this magazine. Do ask at your local Christian bookshop, or contact us direct for details of other BRF Lent titles.

And finally

Thank you once again for all your support for BRF. We look forward to seeing many of you at the Service of Thanksgiving in Westminster Abbey on 30 January, and at the other events during the course of the year.

PS You will find the Gift Subscription and Order Forms at the back of the notes.

75th Anniversary Update

To remind you of what is happening and give you new information regarding events and initiatives for the year...

Service of Thanksgiving and Rededication

Thursday 30 January 1997 in Westminster Abbey, London at 12 noon. A few tickets may still be available—contact Westminster Abbey direct for these.

Group Secretary Days

If you are a Group Secretary you should have received details of these with this issue of the notes. If for some reason you haven't received them, please contact the BRF office for details.

Pilgrimage to the Holy Land

There may still be places available. For further details contact the BRF office direct.

Christian Resources Exhibitions

Come and meet BRF authors and staff, find out more about the work of the Fellowship and see the latest new publications.
20-23 May 1997 Sandown Park, Esher, Surrey
23-25 October 1997 G-MEX, Manchester

Bible Sunday

An outline service, drawing from the Service of Thanksgiving in January will be available later in the year. Full details will be included in the September-December 1997 issue of the *Magazine*.

Author Tour

A major author tour is planned for October. Look out for more details in the next issue of the *Magazine*.

Information Pack

This is now available, containing ideas and suggestions for what you might do in your own church or area to celebrate BRF's anniversary and to promote and encourage Bible reading. Contact the BRF office to request your copy.

Video

Regretfully we have had to postpone the planned video about BRF, but hope very much to be able to produce it at a later date.

Souvenir Brochure

A souvenir brochure for the 75th Anniversary is in preparation. Further details to follow.

New Hymns
for BRF's 75th Anniversary

Bishop Timothy Dudley-Smith has written two new hymns to mark the occasion of BRF's 75th Anniversary. These new hymns will both receive their world premier at the Service of Thanksgiving and Rededication in Westminster Abbey on 30 January 1997.

We are delighted to be able to reproduce both hymns in this issue of *The BRF Magazine*. We hope that you will include them in any services of celebration and thanksgiving for BRF's ministry which you may be planning to hold in your own churches during 1997.

God in his wisdom, for our learning

98 98 98
Suggested tune: Fragrance

God in his wisdom, for our learning,
   gave his inspired and holy word:
promise of Christ, for our discerning,
   by which our souls are moved and stirred,
finding our hearts within us burning
   when, as of old, his voice is heard.

Symbol and story, song and saying,
   life-bearing truths for heart and mind,
God in his sovereign grace displaying
   tenderest care for humankind,
Jesus our Lord this love portraying,
   open our eyes to seek and find.

Come then with prayer and contemplation,
   see how in Scripture Christ is known;
wonder anew at such salvation
   here in these sacred pages shown;
lift every heart in adoration,
   children of God by grace alone!

© *Timothy Dudley-Smith*

Teach us to love the Scriptures, Lord

86 86 (CM)
*Suggested tunes: Contemplation, Westminster, Abridge,
St Hugh, St Timothy*

Teach us to love the Scriptures, Lord,
   to read and mark and learn;
and daily in your written word
   the living Word discern.

Your purposes in us fulfil
   as we your promise claim,
who seek to know and do your will
   and learn to love your Name.

When in some dark and cloudy day
   beset by fears we stand,
your word be light upon our way,
   a sword within our hand.

As on your word our spirits feed
   through all its pages shine;
make known yourself to us who read,
   the Bread of life divine.

So shall the treasures of your word
   become as sacred ground;
teach us to love the Scriptures, Lord,
   where Christ is surely found.

© *Timothy Dudley-Smith*

DISCIPLE

Becoming Disciples through Bible Study

'**I**f you make my word your home you will indeed be my disciples' (John 8:31, New Jerusalem Bible).

Disciple is an exciting new initiative now available in the UK through the partnership of The Foundery Press and BRF. Throughout the USA, South America, Australia, Germany, and Korea Disciple has been instrumental in transforming both individuals and entire congregations as they have worked through the course.

While so many churches seem to be more concerned with making *members*, Jesus was concerned with making *disciples*. Disciple provides a framework for people to relate the teaching of the Bible to their discipleship today, equipping them to serve Christ more effectively in whatever circumstances they find themselves both within and outside their congregations.

What is Disciple? Disciple is a 34 session course comprising daily reading assignments for the individual participant (approx 30 minutes reading per day) plus a 2½-hour weekly group session. The model for the group is twelve members

One minister described Disciple as 'the course I have been looking all my ministry to find.'

plus a leader, who is there as a leader/participant, rather than a leader/teacher.

Disciple requires a high level of commitment from both leader and participants. It is not to be entered into lightly, but has been found to be immensely rewarding by those who have taken part. In the UK a number of pilot schemes have been completed during the last two years, and all involved have spoken of how much they have gained from the course. One minister described Disciple as 'the course I have been looking all my ministry to find.'

Disciple takes the Bible as the text for study. During the course of the 34 weeks participants will read almost 70 per cent of the Old and New Testaments, large sections of which may be for the first time. There are 16 sessions on the Old Testament, one on the intertestamental period and 15 sessions on the New Testament. The final two sessions are for identification of ministry and leadership roles and for celebration of Holy Communion.

For many Christians, their knowledge of and exposure to the Bible is limited to small sections—fragments—the few verses a day in their daily notes, or the reading in church on Sunday. Disciple provides a framework for the reader to understand the broad sweep of the Bible—the 'big picture'. It takes us through the biblical story from Creation to the New Jerusalem, the unfolding story of God's relationship with his people. Each week a different 'Mark of Discipleship' is considered as we relate the themes and implications of what we are reading to our discipleship today.

Each member of the group has a study manual which includes all the daily reading assignments, along with commentary and questions for reflection and response. At the weekly study session the group will watch a video segment which comprises a presentation relevant to the week's study from an acknowledged expert in the field. This is followed by an exploration of the Bible passages which have been read during the preceding week. This will draw on the notes, insights and reflections

Each one of us in the group found ourselves gaining new insights into familiar stories and passages

which participants have recorded during their own reading. A short refreshment break follows after which there is an in-depth study of one passage drawn from the week's readings. Participants are introduced to a number of different Bible study approaches over the 34 sessions and discover techniques which they will be able to apply elsewhere in their own Bible study. Finally the group meeting ends with a consideration of the week's 'Mark of Discipleship' (see above).

Many have asked how Disciple fits in with or relates to the popular Alpha course, which so many churches are now using to great effect throughout the UK and in more and more countries overseas. In our view Disciple and Alpha sit ideally side by side. Alpha is an excellent resource for evangelism and outreach which explains what the Christian faith is all about. Disciple enables people who are already Christians to go deeper into the Bible and to explore issues of biblical discipleship. Ideally churches would offer both courses!

On a personal note, I would not be prepared to promote Disciple had I not actually participated in a Disciple group myself. Between *continued on page 18*

13

Prebendary Douglas Cleverley Ford

Douglas Cleverley Ford died on 4 May 1996. He was a much loved contributor to *New Daylight* from 1989 until his death—and his last notes appear in this issue. When he wrote about the death of his wife, Olga, he had over a hundred letters from people expressing their sympathy and saying how how much that particular note had helped them. You will find it on the last day of this issue of *New Daylight*.

Obituaries appeared in *The Times*, *The Telegraph* and *The Independent*. The following is an extract from the latter, by The Right Reverend The Lord Coggan.

'During a ministry of nearly 60 years he served his generation well—mainly in four spheres.

'The first was as a parish priest... he built up the congregations by the excellence of his preaching... by his insistence on good music, and by his pastoral skill. People knew that if they went to him, especially if they were in trouble or perplexity, they would find a listening ear and an understanding mind. They knew

He did more than any other man of his generation in raising the standard of preaching in the Church of England.

that they mattered—to him and to God.

'Secondly, he worked as a theological college lecturer and as the first Honorary Director of the College of Preachers... Many hundreds of clergy as well as Readers have him to thank for his care, for the lucidity of his lectures, and for the renewal of their preaching work. He did more than any other man of his generation in raising the standard of preaching in the Church of England.

'The third sphere in which he excelled was as senior chaplain to the Archbishop of Canterbury (1975–80). During my years in that office I benefited greatly from his work... He had a shrewd assessment of character. He was loved by the the staff at Lambeth, and his secretaries would do anything for him.

'His fourth skill was as a writer. Over many years, he wrote prolifically, bearing in mind those to whom he had lectured. He desired to enable preachers to do their work with honesty and enthusiasm and to enlist all the help at their disposal in making preaching what it is intended to be—intelligent, interesting, down to earth. The influence of his writings, however, went far beyond the men and women in the pulpit. Through his books...

through articles, through the notes he constantly wrote for the Bible Reading Fellowship, he reached many thousands of readers.

'As a man, he was quiet. Like the Servant in Isaiah, he did "not cry, nor lift up, nor cause his voice to be heard in the street". He did not need to. Some would say he was reserved; but those who knew him best enjoyed his deliciously keen sense of humour which lightened many a difficult situation.'

Douglas will be very much missed by BRF readers.

Shelagh Brown

Douglas Cleverley Ford often wrote notes on the Psalms for *New Daylight*, and shortly before he died BRF published his *Day by Day with the Psalms*.

'The Psalms grew out of life,' he wrote in his introduction, 'and life as we know it is never smooth for long. So the experience of God which they share with us is fragmentary, earthy and human. But as a result we can come alongside the Psalms. We can feel them, sing them and sigh over them... The Psalms are distillatons of life—its joy, its wonder, its laughter, its pain, its loneliness and its fear. They are about living and about dying. It is no wonder they have lasted so long. They have never worn out and they never will.

'The aim of this book is to help the Psalms to address our own individual and contemporary condition, and above all to sharpen and deepen our awareness of the real presence of God in the bitter-sweet knocking about which we know as life.'

The Vision of God (part 3)

Joy Tetley

The biblical presentation of God is kaleidoscopic rather than definitive. The more we look, the more the patterns change. That leaves us in our proper place: wondering; grappling with poetry, mystery and paradox rather than presuming to try and control the great enigma who is God. To try to control God is to try to make ourselves greater than God. That is the primal human sin. And it seriously distorts our vision of who God is.

In safeguarding God's uniqueness, mystery and freedom, the biblical record, when speaking of God, is full of checks and balances. Not least among these is the rich variety of imagery used by the biblical writers. Their metaphors for God are strikingly diverse, often tumbling over one another in a way that throws up many perspectives, many questions. The God of the Scriptures will not be pinned down—except, briefly, on a Cross.

But that dark moment is, in reality, God's brightest beam of light. The God who is beyond our comprehension goes to extremes to make himself known. In a disfigured victim, battling to the end against pain, evil and death, is the focal self-revelation of God—a God whose love for us means more than life itself.

But there is more. As St John puts it, 'in the place where he was crucified there was a garden' (John 19:41). Gardens seem to be significant in the biblical record of God's dealing with us. According to Genesis, human life began in a garden. So did human deceitfulness. There are hints in Revelation of a garden in the city of fulfilment— suggested in the fruitfulness of trees bordering on the river of life (Revelation 22:1–2). And between beginning and ending, we find, for example, cultivated gardens where desire has been aroused (Song of Songs 4:15–16), and cultivated areas where God is portrayed as the gardener (John 15:1).

Now, in what seems the most unlikely place to produce any vision of God, opposite extremes are somehow brought together. Somehow the place of stark horror becomes the place of new life and fruitfulness. Out of darkness and suffering is born a new beginning. This Easter garden, grown out of evil and anguish, is far more fertile than primal Eden. Here love triumphs over hate, forgiveness breaks through the negative spiral of vengeance, joy emerges through pain, life conquers death—not in wishful thinking, but in God's reality. In that reality we can all share; for God does not keep his life to himself. He invites us into it.

It is Christ crucified who takes our pain seriously. It is Christ crucified who, with tortured hands, opens the gate of glory. It is Christ crucified, risen and ascended who ensures that our precious and brittle humanity is for ever at the heart of God.

To this God let us open our eyes anew. Let us 'look to Jesus.' Let us 'see' Jesus. Let us share Jesus. For, as the preacher of Hebrews so powerfully asserts, 'seeing Jesus' means looking into God's life. 'Seeing Jesus' means not only recognizing the presence of God, but being drawn into a face-to-face and heart-to-heart relationship with God. And that also means judgement, in its most radical, and ultimately positive, sense.

Seeing Jesus brings the truth to light—the truth of God and the truth about ourselves. In such mutual openness, we discover the reality of our salvation. We discover that we are loved and forgiven; more—that we are invited to be lovers of God. We discover that our wounds, meeting with God's wounds, can not only find understanding and relief, but even become a source of blessing—for others as well as for ourselves.

We discover that in God's eyes, we have enormous potential for creativity and joy; that, as partners of God, it is our duty, our delight and our travail to bring the best out of all that is; that in the enormity of existence, we matter. As Paul puts it, writing to the Church in Corinth, 'It is the God who said, "Let light shine out of darkness", who has shone in our hearts to give the light of the knowledge of the glory of God in the face of Jesus Christ' (2 Corinthians 4:6).

And what strange glory: hidden, vulnerable, yet carrying the unlimited power of absolute love. Tellingly and typically, the most

Somehow the place of stark horror becomes the place of new life and fruitfulness.

profound insight into this glory comes from the most unexpected quarter. As Mark so shockingly reminds us, it is a pagan outsider, one who is not a member of the chosen people, one who has none of the advantage of discipleship, one who is, quite literally, instrumental in crucifying Jesus, who, in facing this tortured figure dying in less than silent agony, perceives the presence of God.

God grant that we, to whom much has been given, may have the nerve and the strength to affirm that insight. And to go on to share the biblical vision of God with others, in the conviction that this God is powerfully and fundamentally on our side. Being open to such a God is the prelude to transforming grace.

Joy Tetley

Joy Tetley has written Hosea–Micah *in the People's Bible Commentary.*

---

continued from page 13
October 1995 and June 1996 I led a pilot Disciple group with twelve members of my own Anglican church in Oxfordshire. It was a fascinating and exciting journey. Each one of us in the group found ourselves gaining new insights into familiar stories and passages, and discovering parts of the Bible that we had never read before. The sense of anticipation as we came to read Matthew's Gospel in the light of sixteen weeks spent focusing on the Old Testament was almost tangible. And one of the most important things that members of the group without exception felt Disciple had given them was the overview, the framework, with which to understand, approach and explore the Bible. Quite simply, the time spent with Disciple is an investment for life, and wherever you are in your Christian faith, Disciple will equip you for a journey with the Bible that will last the rest of your life.

Disciple is not available through retail outlets. Churches must enrol in the programme and the enrolment fee includes two days' residential training for the group leader, along with all the materials necessary for the first group of twelve to study Disciple. For further details of the course and the training seminars planned for 1997, please send an A5 sae clearly marked 'Disciple' in the top left hand corner to BRF in Oxford.

Richard Fisher

THE ULTIMATE HOLIDAY CLUB GUIDE

The school holidays provide an ideal opportunity to open your church to children of all ages at a time when they are most likely to be at a loose end and looking for entertainment for themselves and their friends.

Holiday clubs are a popular way to use the opportunity to the best advantage. They can be run on a scale to suit your church and the help you have available. But how to start? It's easy to be frightened off by the thought of keeping youngsters occupied, interested and coming back for more.

Here's an ideas-packed guide with all you need to get your holiday club going with a bang. It contains all the information you need to prepare, plan and put together a full programme of events based on a variety of biblical themes—the ideas spring from a wide number of field-tested ventures—plus three complete ready-to-run themes. So whether you are a large inner-city church or a small rural chapel, looking for fresh ideas or on your own wondering where to start, there is something here for you.

The authors have both had extensive experience in working with children at Christian camps and clubs. **Alan Charter** is a full-time youth and children's worker in a busy parish. He met **John Hardwick** whilst working on the Saltmine Children's Team. John has a unique combination of gifts and skills—unicycling, juggling, clowning, music and story-telling—which he uses to present the good news of Jesus Christ imaginatively in ways which appeal to children of all ages.

The Ultimate Holiday Club Guide puts everything you need to know at your fingertips, ready to leap off the page and into your church. Just add a pinch of planning, a dash of enthusiasm, then fill with kids and bring to the boil!

WHY? WHERE? WHAT? WHEN?

A comprehensive section on running a holiday club including:
• initial planning
• roles and responsibilities check list
• using the Bible
• using visual techniques
• using music
• using your imagination
• following up.

HOW to do it!

Three complete holiday club themes, each containing five full days of material including:
- setting the programme
- crafts
- games
- puppetry
- clowning
- theme illustrations
- serial dramas
- creative narrations of Bible passages
- theme songs
- memory verses
- funsheets with photocopy permission
- sheet music.

The Big Top

Five power-packed days exploring the characteristics of God; looking at God's strength, God's love, God's power, God's faithfulness & God's leadership.

The Adventure Cruise

Five fun-filled days on the high 'C's; exploring Choice, Call, Change, Commitment & Cost.

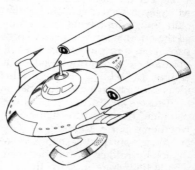

Starship Discovery

Five life-changing days with Peter; exploring Turning, Trusting, Tripping, Transforming & Training.

The book bubbles with enthusiasm.
Together with Children

The three programmes are well presented, full of useful craft ideas, music and worksheets with a serial story to keep the youngsters in suspense until the next morning.
Chelmsford Diocese

It all sounds like such easily achievable fun, you'll be raring to get started.
Parentwise

The cassette is... not just a tape but an exciting and proven way for children to learn.
Christian Bookstore Journal

THE ULTIMATE HOLIDAY CLUB CASSETTE

Contains all the songs and memory verses for the three themes. Ideal for use during your club or as a learning resource, and for your children to take away with them as a memento of their holiday club experience. Side One contains all the songs, Side Two the backing tracks, to help you create that 'singalong-live' atmosphere if you don't have your own musicians.

At BRF our aim is to help *you* help your children to grow with the Bible. We hope you'll find the *Ultimate Holiday Club Guide* and cassette a resource to use and to come back to.

Barnabas, an imprint of the Bible Reading Fellowship

The Barnabas imprint from BRF provides resources to help children under 11 years of age explore, enjoy and begin to learn from the Bible.

To obtain a copy of *The Ultimate Holiday Club Guide*, or copies of the cassette, contact your local Christian bookshop or use the order form on page 159.

The Christian Life
Beginning at the End: the Way of Prayer which Jesus taught us

Simon Barrington-Ward

1. Our Father

Whenever Jesus meets with people, whether in the Gospel stories or now, amongst our contemporaries, he opens up a new possibility. There is such a strong positive sense of being loved and forgiven that you can be overwhelmed by an urge to throw in your lot with his kingdom community and to follow him. Every clause of the prayer which he taught us starts out from this sense of being grasped by God's overwhelming love and thus made ready, like St Paul, to reach out to grasp that for which Christ Jesus has already grasped me (Philippians 3:12).

At the outset, Jesus in Luke's version sets the single word 'Father'. This seems so like him. He immediately invites us to join him in that intimate, trusting relationship with God which he expressed in the word 'Abba', used by children in speaking to their father. This was his most intimate cry to God overheard in the Garden of Gethsemane in the midst of his agony (Matthew 12:24). He must have dwelt within this word himself. In this naked dwelling, he endured utter godforsakenness on the cross to break through death to a release of the Spirit into the hearts of all who turn to him, so that we too can confidently cry with him 'Abba'.

Matthew embellishes it with the traditional 'Our' and 'in heaven' to remind us that it is the prayer of the new covenant community, now held in unity with God.

All our prayers should start with remembering God's great love for us to which we are brought home through Jesus by the Spirit. We start by dwelling on this thought. It is then that we can long and struggle to become what we truly are.

2. Hallowed be your name...

As we really dwell in that sense of being loved and accepted just as we are and brought home to God, thankfulness and praise can well up from us. We want to be caught up into heaven in praising him and to see the world charged with his glory. We have arrived at the end. Heaven and earth are one and all creation shouts its praise.

But then again our joy is turned into longing. May your name be made holy. The prophets longed for this and felt that God's name was profaned through the failure of his people to live their praise out. (Isaiah 29:23, Ezekiel 36:23). Jesus prayed 'Glorify your name!' (John 12:28). But he knew that that prayer could only be fulfilled in the face of the failure of God's people in a sinful world if he were to lay down his life so as to raise up a new people. We too can only pray this if we are willing to take up his cross in our lives.

3. Your Kingdom come, (Your will be done, on earth as in heaven).

Again when Jesus prays this prayer the kingdom of heaven, the sovereign rule of God over everything, seems to be at hand. We begin to picture it. The torn creation made whole. A new kind of human society. A community, and even our own hearts united with God. Matthew amplifies the prayer again by adding 'Your will be done in earth as in heaven' and we remember once again that Jesus prayed this prayer in Gethsemane, 'Nevertheless not my will but yours' (Matthew 26:39). Only through our surrender and repentance can this prayer, fulfilled already in Jesus, begin to be fulfilled in us. Once again we move from the joy of the picture of the kingdom close at hand in Jesus to the yearning that God's will might be done not only in him but in us. We can pray then another very early version of this clause, 'May your Holy Spirit come upon us and cleanse us...' As our repentance for our own failure and our intercessions for the world fuse into one great longing, so we seek to open ourselves to the presence of the Holy Spirit who alone can begin to fulfil this prayer.

4. Give us today tomorrow's bread...

Here Matthew's version has that original ring. The mysterious word translated in our modern versions 'daily', *'epiousion'* really means 'for the morrow'. It could be a prayer to rest secure tonight knowing that tomorrow's bread was there. But there is an echo of the manna that fell in the desert, when God gave enough for two days to cover the Sabbath. The Sabbath itself being a sign of the end time and the last day. There is a glimpse too of the feeding of the five thousand which was both a memory of the manna and an anticipation of the final feast of which Jesus often spoke. The bread of the morrow must be shared bread, bread broken in a longing for Jesus' coming. Each meal becomes, as for Quakers, a sacrament. We enter into the final feast already, but also we must struggle to share amongst each other bread and all material things if w are to know the joy of our true fulfilment to come.

5. Forgive (remit) us our debts, as we have forgiven our debtors...

Here too we are, thanks to the passion and death of Jesus, freed from sin and brought into that final state in which all is being forgiven and forgiving. We have passed beyond the judgment, from death to life and into universal love. 'We have forgiven' our debtors already. There is a kind of general amnesty, a jubilee in which all sin has been cleansed away. And yet again we are not there yet. We need still to be grasped by forgiveness and also to be reaching out to forgive. Forgiveness is all we have. It is the central theme of the kingdom community. It is the way to the kingdom. That is why Matthew attaches such importance to this clause. Only through continuous forgiveness, love for our enemies, the love that drives out fear, can humankind reach its final fulfilment in God.

Forgiveness is all we have.

6. Lead us not into temptation (but deliver us from the evil one)

In this prayer, held in God's presence and love and in the final joy, we are secured and taken beyond the greatest temptation of all, to lose hold of God. We are taken beyond the trial of tragedy and suffering and death which can detach us from faith at the crucial moment. 'Suffer us not for any pangs of death to fall from you!' In Matthew's extra clause we pray to be delivered from the evil one, which is surely the more authentic and earliest reading. Our vulnerable little community of love prays to be protected from the mystery of iniquity and the great destruction constantly let loose in this world. We are held in a love which 'bears all things, believes all things, hopes all things, endures all things'. And yet, paradoxically we must keep reaching out in faith to God in Christ or we shall lose that delicate poise of grace.

7. Doxology

It is surely true to the prayer that some ancient manuscripts in Matthew's version, as in the later document called the 'Didache' or 'Teaching', add 'for yours is the kingdom, and the power and the glory, for ever. Amen', with it strong echo of Judaic tradition, especially 1 Chronicles 29:11. This, though not part of the original, surely returns us to the end, which we know already as we dwell in God's love and rest in faith and hope. 'The last thing is a joy, a joy that rejoices out of an ever new joy in eternity.'

In all our prayer and life in Christ we learn to dwell in the end which he has won on his cross, the end which is now and not yet, and so to reach out for it daily. We cry 'Glorify your name, bring your kingdom, let your will be done in us.' And as we seek these things, we are led through shared bread, forgiven and forgiving and a constant deliverance, towards the still unseen fulfilment of our prayer.

Searching for Truth

From the introduction to John Polkinghorne's book

A Scientist's Approach

Whatever it is that we do in life, the experiences we have will colour our thoughts and mould our ways of thinking. I have spent thirty years of my life working as a theoretical physicist, trying to use mathematics to understand some of the beautiful patterns and order of the physical world. For good or ill (and no doubt it is a mixture of both) this affects how I think about all sorts of things. The way I like to characterise my habits of thought is to say that I am a 'bottom-up' thinker.

What I mean by that is that I like to start with the phenomena, with things that have happened, and then try to build up an explanation and an understanding from there. 'Start with particular cases and only then try to go on to understand what's happening in general' is my motto. If you're a 'top-down' thinker, you like to go the other way: start with some grand general ideas and use them to explain particular events.

Bottom-up thinking is natural for a scientist for two reasons. One is that we are looking for ideas which have reasons backing them up, and these reasons will lie in the evidence we consider, the events that motivate our belief. The second point is that we have learnt that the world is full of surprises. That means it is very hard to guess beforehand what the right general ideas will turn out to be. Only experience can tell us that. In fact, this element of surprise is one of the things that makes scientific research worthwhile and exciting. You never know what you'll find round the next corner.

Let me give you just one example of these scientific surprises. Every day of my working life as a theoretical physicist I use the ideas of quantum mechanics. This theory describes how things behave on a very small scale, the size of atoms or even smaller. It turns out that the behaviour of the very small is totally different from the way we experience the world on the feet-and-inches scale of everyday life. We seem to live in a world which is reliable and picturable. We know where things are and what they are doing. All that changes when you get down to the level of atoms. Take an electron, one of the constituents of an atom. If you know where it is, you cannot know what it is doing; if you know what it is doing, you cannot know where it is! (This is called Heisenberg's uncertainty principle.) The quantum world is fuzzy and unpicturable. We cannot imagine in everyday terms what it is like. Nevertheless we can understand it, using mathematics and the special set of quantum ideas which we have learnt about from a bottom-up approach to atomic phenomena.

No one could have guessed beforehand that matter would behave in this very odd way when looked at subatomically. In fact it took many extremely clever people twenty-five years to figure out what was happening. If you want to understand nature, you have to let the physical world tell you what it's like. You have to start at the bottom, with actual behaviour, and work your way up to an adequate theory.

Now, if the physical world is so full of surprises, it would be strange if God didn't also exceed our expectations in quite unexpected ways. Commonsense thinking by itself won't be adequate to tell us what he's like. We'll have to try to find out from how he has actually made himself known. That's why I was keen in the preceding section to think of the Bible as a source of evidence about how God has acted in history and, above all, in Jesus Christ. It's a natural strategy for a bottom-up thinker to pursue.

You'll see, in fact, that I find there's a lot in common between the way I search for truth in science and the way I search for truth in religion. People are sometimes surprised that I'm both a physicist and a priest. They think there's something odd, or maybe even dishonest, in the combination. Their surprise arises because they don't realize that truth matters quite as much in religion as it does in science. There is an odd

view around that faith is a matter of shutting one's eyes, gritting one's teeth and believing impossible things because some unquestionable authority tells you that you have to. Not at all! The leap of faith is a leap into the light and not into the dark. It involves commitment to what we understand in order that we may learn and understand more. You have to do that in science. You have to trust that the physical world makes sense and that your present theory gives you some sort of idea of what it's like, if you are to make progress and gain more understanding and a better theory. You'll never see anything if you don't stick your neck out a bit! You have to do the same in the religious quest for truth. We shall never have God neatly packaged up. He will always exceed our expectations and prove himself to be a God of surprises. There is always more to learn.

There is one important difference, however, between scientific belief and religious belief. The latter is much more demanding and more dangerous. I believe passionately in quantum theory, but the belief doesn't threaten to change my life in any significant way. I cannot believe in God, however, without knowing that I must be obedient to his will for me as it becomes known to me. God is not there just to satisfy my intellectual curiosity; he is there to be honoured and respected as my Creator and Saviour. Beware! Let me utter a theological health warning or, rather, promise: 'Reading the Bible can change your life'.

26

The Apple of His Eye

An extract from the BRF book by Bridget Plass

John 11:28–29, 32–35

After she had said this she went back and called her sister aside. 'The teacher is here' she said 'and is asking for you.' When Mary heard this she got up quickly and went to him... When Mary reached the place where Jesus was and saw him she fell at his feet and said, 'Lord if you had been here my brother would not have died.'

When Jesus saw her weeping and the Jews who had come along with her also, he was deeply moved in spirit and troubled. 'Where have you laid him?' he asked. 'Come and see Lord,' they replied.

Jesus wept.

Why? Why did he weep? Surely he knew that everything was going to be all right for his favourite family?

Was it because he felt guilty that he could have prevented their pain by coming earlier but because he needed Lazarus' healing to be a major miracle they had had to suffer? Or because he knew that what he was about to do was the beginning of his own long journey towards death? Or because he knew, as God's Son, that whatever he said they could not understand. Or quite simply because he was truly man while he was with us and couldn't bear to see his dear friends in such agony. Whatever the reason I'm so very glad he did.

Sometimes, especially since being a parent, I've found myself in a situation where I've known that someone's grief will only be temporary. I've plastered grazed knees and tried unsuccessfully to mend favourite toys; I've cuddled to sleep a toddler devastated by the loss of a one eared rabbit, I've attended funerals of budgies and hamsters; I've watched helplessly the agony caused by the betrayal of a best friend who chooses to sit next to someone else on the coach; I've touched fingers in sympathy at an unsuccessful audition; I've listened to the thudding grief of a small mud plastered footballer who has just scored an own goal. And I've been there myself.

I've learnt slowly that passing on knowledge that their grief will be temporary in the form of 'Never mind. You'll get over it' is useless and can be damaging. Yes the pain will lessen in time, may even go completely. But right now they are hurting and they can't understand and nothing will ever be the same again.

If you are in that situation now, needing arms round you and needing to know that someone who loves you is sitting in the dark with you, remember that Jesus wept. He knew he was going to heal Lazarus, but still he wept. He will never minimise your pain. Just as he was asking for Mary who had shut herself away from everyone in her grief, so he is asking for you. Let him weep with you.

PRAYER

Oh Father you know us so well. You know the pain that is bleeding its way through our heads and hearts. You know the panic and loneliness that comes about from feeling that there is no one who can or who wants to understand. Help us to uncurl from our dark corner and turn to you. Help us to tell you all the little things that she or he said, or didn't say. Help us to look at you so we can see your tears.

BRF's Lent books for 1997, *Searching for Truth* by John Polkinghorne and *The Apple of His Eye* by Bridget Plass are available from your local Christian bookshop or, in case of difficulty, direct from BRF. See order form on page 159.

The Immanence of God

John Fenton

The first-century Jewish historian Josephus tells us that the robes that the High Priest had to wear at the great festivals in the temple in Jerusalem were kept by the Romans in the Tower of Antonia.

The dates of the festivals were fixed according to the sighting of the new moon, and the vestments had to be taken to the High Priest a week before the holy day to ensure that they were ritually clean: so presumably someone had to go from the High Priest's house to the Antonia to collect the robes, or at least to remind the Romans that they were needed.

The High Priest could not perform his duties without the appropriate vestments.

Which things (one might say) are an allegory. For us, it is not a long blue robe with bells and pomegranates that we need, but our real, true self, free from selfishness and fear, envy and all artificiality. It is not kept in a stone tower in Jerusalem, but with God.

We have to go to him, to get what we need, if we are ever to do his will. Not one, nor even three or four times a year (as with the Jewish festivals and the Day of Atonement) but more frequently than that— every day, every moment.

There is an experience that everybody knows: Something has got into me; I am not myself today. In order to do certain complicated actions—in sport, or in the theatre, or in society—one has first to become inwardly aware of what one is going to do: the gymnast stands waiting on the edge of the mat; the actor in the dressing-room gets into the part; the speaker waits for the cue, collecting the whole matter together before beginning to speak.

Being ourselves and doing what has to be done are not with us automatically and all the time. We have to fetch our real self from somewhere else. Without it, we cannot do the thing properly, whatever it is.

The writers of the New Testament knew this, too, and described it in terms of what you wear. They wrote about putting off the old nature, and putting on Christ, or the armour of God, or faith and love and hope. Your life, Paul said to the Colossians, is hidden from you; it is with Christ, in God (3:2).

We cannot do what we believe

29

we should do, unless we can collect what we need to do it with; we cannot be ourselves, because our self is not permanently and automatically at our disposal. We cannot assume that we have it by us; it must be fetched; and that takes time.

The 'me' that I need is, in one sense, not me at all. Certainly this was Paul's experience; It is no longer I who live, but it is Christ who lives in me (Galatians 2:20).

It would be a mistake to take this for granted, and live as though I did not need to remember it, and do it. Some things one need not usually remember: to keep on breathing, for example; to sleep and rise, night and day.

But collecting ourselves is not like that; it requires the deliberate and conscious act of asking, going out, fetching, putting on, adjusting, checking to see that it is the right way round.

The New Testament writers say the same thing in another way, too. They and their first readers saw themselves as containers that needed to be filled, or rather, that needed to be emptied first, and then filled. You might be full of wickedness, of the evil forces that they called unclean spirits, demons, Beelzebul. What you needed was to be filled with goodness, kindness, Christ, the Spirit, God.

What we are is always potential, something to be developed, not yet attained, not yet what it should be and shall be.

God is the fulness, with which he will complete all his creatures. We have hardly any idea what this will mean for the other things he made, but we have an inkling how it will be for us; we can just about imagine what it might be like to be filled with God.

To get there, there will have to be two elements: one negative, the other positive. The destruction of the false self, and the receiving of the true self. They are like Babylon and Jerusalem in the Revelation. Dying and rising. Emptying out and being filled. Taking off one set of clothes and putting on another. Turning away and turning towards.

Of course what is to be received and longed for and accepted is infinitely better than what is to be abandoned—the familiar, unattractive me.

What we are on the way towards is God himself, fulfilling us, as he will fulfil everything that he has made. He will be everything, to every body; all, in all.

John Fenton *was formerly Principal of St Chad's College, Durham and a Canon of Christ Church in Oxford. He is the author of* The Matthew Passion, *published by BRF, which is available from your local Christian bookshop or, in case of difficulty, direct from BRF. See order form, page 159.*

Selected Psalms

The Psalter has been used for centuries by Jewish and Christian congregations and individuals to enrich their public worship and private devotion. On the one hand, it was realized that the devotional language of the Psalms was so simple that generation after generation of ordinary people could appreciate their treasures, while on the other hand the richness of their ideas was so full that even the most able scholars found it impossible to plumb their depths. The hymns and prayers of the Psalter describe all the fluctuations of the human spirit—lamentation and praise, sadness and joy, hate and love, spiritual pride and humble submission—and every transient emotion is contrasted with the majesty of the unchanging Saviour-God. In the Psalms we encounter a wrestling with mankind's age-old problems such as the prosperity of the wicked, the agonizing fear of death, persecution by cruel enemies, the suffering of the innocent, and the whole meaning of life itself. The worshippers ascend the temple mount, and through its Psalms try to offer their requests before God by utilizing the liturgies, hymns and prayers prepared for their use by the sanctuary's poets.

Recent scholarship has clearly shown that the temple and its services form the natural home of Israel's Psalms. It was the duty of the temple officials to sing them 'skilfully' and the personnel included experts in poetry and musicianship. David in particular was renowned as 'the sweet psalmist of Israel' (2 Samuel 23:1) and it is generally agreed that the Psalter on the whole preserves the work of the specialists in psalmody and its accompanying music. They knew the deepest needs of the temple worshippers and prepared Psalms especially on their behalf in the language idioms peculiar to Israel's religious traditions.

These notes are based on the Revised English Bible.

1–5 JANUARY   THE WAY AHEAD

1   **True blessedness; choosing between two ways**   *Read Psalm 1*

The main theme of the first Psalm is the happiness of the righteous and the destruction of the wicked. This happiness is emphasized in such a way that no translation can really do it justice. The full experience of inward happiness and outward felicity of the opening words greets us when we encounter 'Happy is the one...', yet the same version renders the Greek equivalent in Matthew's account of the Sermon on the Mount as 'blessed'. The really righteous person is impossible to describe adequately in any vocabulary. The righteous and 'happy' are seen as the friends of God, and the wicked are those who are God's enemies. The Psalm opposes the false principle that the wicked flourish and the righteous suffer unduly. The wicked are described in three different ways in verse 1. The procession 'walk, stand, sit' is not merely Hebrew poetic style; it shows a deepening sense of evil, the ultimate settling down to the easy evasions of mockery. After this negative approach we are led to a far more positive sphere, that of showing delight in God's law.

The poet closes with a graphic depiction of the difference between the two ways as seen in the Psalm. The way of the righteous is safe, for God watches over them, but the wicked are left to their own devices and doomed (v. 6). Their 'way' is simply a path that finally peters out.

This Psalm was probably deliberately chosen as an opening poem for the Psalter: it is also an apt reading for the opening of a new year.

2   True protection; the shepherd   *Read Psalm 23*

This Psalm has often been called 'The Psalm of Psalms' and is better known than any other part of scripture except for the Lord's Prayer. Despite its well-known phrases it is worth looking at afresh because it is a personal confession of faith in true protection from a God who cares for his people.

The picture of God as shepherd is not confined to this Psalm. 'He shall feed his flock like a shepherd', says Isaiah 40:11 (see also Jeremiah 23:3; Ezekiel 34:11–16; Psalm 80:1). It is a metaphor also used to describe the king, especially David the shepherd lad who led his people (2 Samuel 5:2; 7:7; Psalm 78:70–72). The picture of the king as a shepherd is not confined to Israelite theology: many of the neighbouring nations thought of their leaders and gods as shepherds of their people.

The usual reciting or singing in the temple of the national history-of-salvation, which celebrated God's acts in protecting his people through their past, is applied in this Psalm to God's care for the individual. Each one is of value to God (see Psalm 103:13).

Verses 2–4 describe the care and leadership of the shepherd. Leading rather than driving the flock is the usual practice of the oriental shepherd. The picture also shows the flock being 'revived' and ready to continue the journey after enjoying the pleasant pastures and restful waters. As the Psalm continues, the fact that it speaks of God's care and protection becomes clearer for, like the shepherd, he must lead his people through the dark ravines of life's dangers. The worshipper feels safe with God even in the darkest experiences of life.

Many interpreters feel that in verses 5–6 the picture changes. It moves from the description of the opening verses to addressing God directly. We see God as the welcoming host offering gracious hospitality. The worshipper rejoices in the fact that the deep experiences of fellowship found in God's house can be enjoyed continuously in the ordinary round of life.

3 True prayer; addressing the holy God   *Read Psalm 99*

This Psalm pivots on declaring the holiness of God and has been assigned by most commentators to the liturgy of Israel's New Year Festival when God's enthronement, his dispensation of justice, execution of vengeance and his forgiveness were celebrated. The theme of God's holiness is highlighted in the refrain of verses 3, 5 and 9 which gets progressively longer.

The first section (vv. 1–3) opens with an acknowledgment of God's sovereignty and our appropriate response in worship. God is the universal King, and the trembling of the people at his awesome presence is accompanied by earth's shaking. The people are called to pray and worship this most holy and exalted God.

The second section (vv. 4–5) also opens with a reference to God's kingship but this time he is to be acknowledged as the God of righteousness and justice. His people are summoned to worship at his 'footstool' (v. 5), an expression used in various ways of God enthroned. It represents Mount Zion (Isaiah 60:13; Ezekiel 43:7), the earth itself (Isaiah 66:1; Matthew 5:35) but it is most likely that the Psalmist is referring to the ark of the covenant (see 1 Chronicles 28:2; Psalm 132:7).

In the third section (vv. 6–9) God's covenant people are exhorted to prayer, and the religious heroes of Israel's past are cited as examples of correct attitudes in prayer. Their priestly ministry of intercession is emphasized. Yet, this is no mere return to past history, for the same God who heard and answered the prayers of Moses, Aaron and Samuel, will also answer the prayers of the present congregation. This living relationship between God and his people cannot be confined to the past for God is faithful in every generation which offers true prayer to the true God. Israel discovers God in punishment as well as love, in judgment as well as grace. The Psalm closes with the solemn refrain acknowledging God's holiness and his relationship to his people; he is 'the Lord *our* God'.

4 True freedom; God's freedom   *Read Psalm 66*

In characteristic style the Psalm opens on a joyful note with a general call for the whole world to worship God. This call is confirmed by the use of four imperatives within the first three short sentences (vv. 1–3). Two basic elements shine through, namely giving praise and glory to God.

It has been often suggested that God's mighty acts were presented in the temple in dramatic form and the people invited to 'Come and see what God has done' (v. 5). Two major events in Israel's history-of-salvation are specifically mentioned—the crossing of the Red Sea (Exodus 14:21–22) and the crossing of the River Jordan (Joshua 3:14–17). The escape from Egyptian slavery and possession of Canaan as a homeland were seen as the two great historical acts by which God brought freedom to his people, and the temple congregation were invited to participate in this experience through worship. The nations are invited to join in praising God for his goodness to his people (vv. 8–12) although Israel's path through history was not always smooth. She was finally given her freedom in a place of plenty (v. 12). It is important to note that this is not a freedom *from* anything as much as a freedom *for* something—freedom to be God's instrument to bring all nations to praise him.

It is against this background that the individual worshippers now offer praise to God for their own personal experience of deliverance (vv. 13–20). Two elements become apparent. First, they must each pay the vows and sacrifice the offerings which they promised to God when they were in dire distress and seeking release from the cause of their grief (vv. 13–15). But this is not all; the good news must be shared. And so strong testimony is given to the God who hears and answers prayer (vv. 16–20). Whether the psalmist's sense of confinement was caused by illness or by sin we are not told, only the plea for freedom and that God has graciously answered as he answered Israel of old. This testimony, ancient though it is, draws us in to share our testimony too that he 'has not withdrawn from me his love and care'.

GUIDELINES

We hear about the difficulties of living today from every quarter. It was no different for the Psalmists in their times. They, like us, were forced to face harsh realities. The appearance of Assyrian or Babylonian war-chariots would have struck as much terror as the appearance of hostile missile-carrying aircraft or nuclear submarines in our time. Fear knows no boundaries.

The Psalmists took their fears and insecurities to God in their worship and sought true solace there through his protection and guidance. They found this stability, comfort and truth in their experience of worship. God was always there for them despite their unfaithfulness towards him. Their God was the God of truth and unchanging faithfulness in the midst of their transient lives. They sought his guidance for the way ahead.

During one of the darkest periods of our present century during the first months of World War II, the British monarch, George VI, in his Christmas broadcast quoted the words of Minnie Louise Haskins: 'And I said to the man who stood at the gate of the year: "Give me a light that I may tread safely into the unknown." And he replied: "Go out into the darkness and put your hand into the hand of God. That shall be to you better than light and safer than a known way."'

6–12 JANUARY   THE TWISTS AND TURNS OF LIFE

1   False companions; such sorry company   Read Psalm 55

This poignant lament preserved in Psalm 55 was seen by older commentators as the work of more than one author. Recent interpreters have offered a different explanation and suggest that the Psalm's grammatical difficulties and leaps in logic are a reflection of the Psalmist's deep emotional strain. His feelings are so mixed up that they burst forth in all sorts of unconnected ways.

The Psalm opens in the typical style of the ancient lament when the petitioner makes his urgent appeal to God and describes his troubles (vv. 1–11). The first two verses are the usual opening plea for a sympathetic hearing from a God who seems to be distant or hiding at that particular moment. This adds to the petitioner's grief. Then in verses 3–5 he offers a more detailed account of his hurts: he is panic-stricken and feels that death's agonies have already overtaken him. The clamour of the wicked deafens him, and the feeling one gets at this point is of one suffering an inward emotional breakdown.

It is no surprise that he seeks an escape (vv. 6–8) either as a dove or a desert nomad whose footsteps are covered by the desert winds; both leave no known tracks.

His petition for deliverance from his enemies now turns him once again to God. He is aware that God is his only true refuge. He now asks God to act as he did in the days of the tower of Babel (Genesis 11:5–9). In those days God mixed, confused and scattered a city full of wickedness. It is obvious that the same faults are now rife in the city of Jerusalem in the Psalmist's day; the holy city itself is so full of moral anarchy.

Verses 12–14 form the first of two sections describing betrayal by a most intimate companion. The petitioner was able to cope with the hatred of enemies as well as their mockery, but the treachery of a friend is as much as he can bear. In verse 14 he tries to remind his friend of their past happiness. Many interpreters have drawn a likeness between this man's actions and those of Judas in the New Testament.

In verses 15–19 the false friend is forgotten for the moment and the Psalmist utilizes much stronger language in requesting drastic action for the removal of his enemies. He desires the earth to open and swallow them and uses language which has echoes of the terrible fate of Korah and his fellow rebels in Numbers 16:30ff; he is in such despair that he prays that they may be taken down to Sheol while they still live, the worst end imaginable. He contrasts the impious behaviour of the enemies with his own piety and devotion which will ensure God's intervention.

He now returns again to reopen the hurtful wound of betrayal (vv. 20–21). Solemn oaths were to be kept at all costs and smooth words do not really hide evil.

The Psalm closes with a proclamation of assurance and comfort.

This statement could be the reassuring word of a temple prophet which the poet has added as a positive conclusion to his prayer (vv. 22–23c), which he reiterates with a final assertion of his deep trust in God (v. 23d).

2 False accusations; a plea for vengeance   Read Psalm 109

This Psalm is a very strong reaction to malicious and false accusations and the severity of its curses has caused its removal from many lectionaries. The fact that the Psalm is difficult to interpret is no grounds for pretending it is not found in the Bible.

The opening lament (vv. 1–5) is followed by a long string of strong curses (vv. 6–19) and it is these that have caused so much difficulty in its interpretation throughout the ages.

This Psalm opens with a poignant appeal for God to help because of the ruthless effects of false accusations. The Psalmist obviously feels the existence of an unjust conspiracy against him and this is reflected in the strong vocabulary of verses 2–3. Their ingratitude is highlighted in verses 4–5 when they are shown to return evil for good and hatred instead of love. *I read this as the Psalmist's view of his enemies*

Verses 6–19 form the longest section and are self-explanatory as the enemies' hatred knows no bounds. They have condemned him before his false trial has even begun. They are not content to destroy him but to obliterate his family also (vv. 13–15). The accusers feel that their cursing is justified and indeed this section provides very difficult reading. Their black notes of despair are counterbalanced only by the Psalmist's vision that only one path lies open to him, and that is to throw his whole being on God's mercy: a lesson that many should take to heart.

He therefore continues with his prayer for help (vv. 20–29) appealing earnestly that the very cursing of his enemies be returned upon them. This in his mind would be just retribution (v. 20) but he then pulls up short and strikes a new note (vv. 22–25) when he describes his sorry plight through lack of food and severe illness. Despite all this, God's blessings will prove far superior to the cursing of the enemies (v. 28).

The concluding stanza is a vow (vv. 30–31) when the worshipper promises to praise God in the temple as he feels assured that God will deliver him.

3 False health; a sufferer's prayer *Read Psalm 38*

Christian tradition has long regarded Psalm 38 as one of the 'Penitential Psalms' (along with Psalms 6, 32, 51, 102, 130 and 143). An additional element (seen to a lesser degree in Psalm 109, above) has been added to the cruel taunts of the petitioner's enemies—and that is suffering a painful and loathsome disease for which he knows no cure. No precise details of the sickness are given but it is obvious that, in accordance with the thought-patterns of his time, he considers his illness direct punishment from God, and sees his social group rejecting him in consequence.

The Psalm opens with an admission of guilt (see Psalm 6:1 for a similar pattern) and in verse 2 he sees his punishment actualized by body-penetrating arrows and the heaviness of God's hand raised against him. The illness is no mere psychosomatic pain or hypochondriac's ailment but a real affliction affecting his whole body (v. 3). He believes that this is God's punishment for his sin and that it is useless to rebel. The severe strain of his guilt and sickness prove far too much for him to bear. Despite describing his wounds (v. 5) and his severe fever (v. 7), even the reference to his illness in verse 11 makes it impossible to diagnose any specific malady on the grounds of such general feelings. Although it is obvious that he is in deep mourning, yet this general vocabulary may be deliberate so that the Psalm would be appropriate for more than one occasion.

The poet does not find much time to dwell on his symptoms; his enemies are already being far more malicious (v. 12). In reality it is not the physical aspects of his illness which cause his greatest concern, but his ostracism from his usual companions and from society in general. It is terrible: friends have turned into enemies, probably out of fear of contamination (we may see parallels with AIDS here), and set traps to remove him from their lives.

In verses 13–20 the sufferer is forced to turn back to God. He does not argue his innocence but declares his impotence in word and deed bluntly and regrettably in verses 13–14.

In verse 15 he declares where his real hope lies and asserts his assurance of an answer to his earnest prayer. He is willing to leave his whole circumstances in the hands of God.

In the concluding verses of the Psalm the poet makes no excuse for his sin, but admits his guilt and confesses in great stress that he cannot endure his suffering for much longer (vv. 17–22). A note of resentment is sounded in verse 19; the petitioner feels bitter because of his adversaries who return evil for good. It is no accident, therefore, that his final plea is a short prayer for the presence and practical assistance of his God (vv. 21–22). It is here that he sees his only hope for salvation. He begs God not to be distant but to be a friend and deliverer. This is a prayer in which every human being should feel involved to the uttermost.

4 False worship; God's temple in ruins   *Read Psalm 74*

This is a very sorry Psalm. It is obvious that a congregation has assembled to worship but finds that God's house has been desecrated, probably through the destruction of the temple and of Jerusalem itself by Nebuchadnezzar in 587BC (see 2 Kings 24). It is not beyond comprehension, however, that this Psalm may have been used at subsequent times of oppression and subjugation by other worldly powers.

The Psalm opens with the usual characteristic of the lament, the poignant question 'why?' (v. 1). The situation is one of tension for the worshippers (vv. 2–3) as they are unable to reconcile their present predicament and failures with the promises of God for his protection and assistance. They are still puzzled regarding God's character and why he has let this terrible calamity overtake them. In their agony they appeal to God to restore to them some of their former glory so that their enemies may not be so blatantly victorious and sneering.

In verses 4–8 the opening plea gives way to a vivid description of events. It is ironic that the enemies' taunts and gestures of victory take place on the very spot where God's people used to offer him praise. It is there that they have chosen to set up their military standards with the conspicuous pagan symbolism as a sign of possession. They wield their axes busily destroying all decorations of wood and metal (see 2 Kings 18:16), putting the temple and other sacred places of assembly to the torch.

Another aspect of the sorry state of the land is presented in verses 9–11 when the congregation are robbed of any testimony or signs of God's presence amongst them. The worshippers are confused with the stilling of the prophetic voice and the voice of praise, and fervently complain against God for his inactivity.

In spite of the drastic conditions of the temple and land, the congregation still declares its faith in God as Creator-King who manifests his sovereignty through creative action and redemptive deeds. Many interpreters see behind verses 14–17 an echo of the creation myths of ancient Canaan and Babylon. The language here is ironic for it is God alone who is the true Creator, and they stress their belief that the God who conquered the watery chaos at the very beginning will emerge as sovereign from the chaos of the present situation.

Before concluding, the congregation make another earnest plea for God to act on their behalf and for the sake of the honour of his name (vv. 18–23). The appeal is to God's covenant for rescue from their enemies especially when they are tracked down and slaughtered in their hiding places. God is reminded that he should not let these enemies be victorious for ever, for his people are part of his honour and glory. The only way to restore this is to quieten the clamour of the cruel enemies.

5   False neighbours; Israel's enemies   *Read Psalm 83*

This Psalm is a community lament suitable for offering during a national calamity. Interpreters are not sure of the exact historical circumstances which gave rise to its cries but perhaps the stereotyped language of the Psalm was deliberate so that it could be used on more than one occasion of national emergency.

The community lament follows the same pattern as that of the lament of the individual in that it opens with a cry for hearing (v. 1) and then states the very grounds for that appeal (vv. 2–8). The neighbouring countries plan a conspiracy against the people of God forming an alliance so that Israel may be destroyed. The very naming of the nations in verses 6–8 could be a traditional method of cursing. These are Israel's near neighbours, enemies at different periods of history, and fused together here probably in order to highlight the dangers which continually threatened Israel. There is no historical record in the biblical books or any extra-biblical evidence of such a widespread alliance against Israel, yet the threat was always there, and Israel was forced to live under its shadow.

Verses 9–18 are a prayer centring on the destruction which God's people would like to see overtake their enemies as in her past history. This prayer is not a magical formula in curse form, but a real appeal to God on the basis of past deliverance from situations when the odds were overwhelmingly against her. Israel possessed these rich traditions of her past history to which she could appeal, and God's people here offer prayer that history may once again repeat itself in her favour.

Another characteristic of Israel's ancient wars was that the elements associated with the manifestation of God's presence, such as storm, fire, and hurricane, terrified the enemies. Verses 14–15 are a prayer for these terrible elements to break out again and produce the same awesome effect. It must be admitted that the prime characteristic which surfaces in this Psalm is the imprecatory spirit of vengeance, although verses 16–18 seek a much higher motive, that 'they may seek your name... let it be known'. The prime motive therefore is for these false neighbours to turn and acknowledge Israel's God, since he alone is worthy of being acknowledged as God of their immediate geographical area and indeed of the whole earth.

6   False gods; and a true judge   *Read Psalm 58*

Psalm 58 is usually seen as a lament of the community because it lacks any personal detail which would tie it with the experience of an individual. It is obvious that the period is one of moral turmoil, although it is impossible to decide on any specific period in Israel's history.

The opening words are an accusation against the wickedness of the 'gods'. The REB tries to get out of this difficulty by translating 'rulers', but there are many places in the Old Testament where heavenly creatures are seen as bearers of responsibilities delegated to them by God. These were often the patron deities of individual nations (see Deuteronomy 32:8). The Psalm uses mythological language and the whole point is that those given the responsibility of ensuring the rule of justice on earth have failed in their obligations.

Verses 3–5 describe the actions of the wicked and many commentators see these verses as reflecting the story of the garden of Eden. Wickedness is seen as rebellion against God and its effects may be compared to the deadly venom of the serpent. Humans are seen here as degenerate tools in the hands of the rebellious 'gods', although this does not absolve them of their own individual responsibility for sin.

It is ironic that the poet uses a sevenfold curse on the wicked in verses 6–9, as seven is usually the number associated with perfection. God is the one who is requested to operate the curses, and these are presented in such a vivid way that there is no need to explain them here.

The Psalm closes with rejoicing and gratitude (vv. 10–11). It is hard for the Christian reader to share the Psalmist's feelings here. Yet we must face reality and realize that people have not always been forgiving even in Christian times and that at least the worshippers want God to execute vengeance rather than undertaking this themselves. The closing declaration asserts that it is God who dispenses justice on earth and no one else.

GUIDELINES

Can there be any justification for reading these old-fashioned songs in today's world? Have these cruel taunts any relevance for the end of the second millennium? We can answer 'Yes' categorically on four counts:

- *because they take sin seriously and make no effort to hide its evil or cruel consequences;*

- *because they have been preserved in the Bible, not as ideals or examples, but as warnings of what humans are capable of inflicting on one another;*

- *because they declare clearly that vengeance is God's prerogative and not for humans—they went to the temple to pray for vengeance, but left it then in God's hands;*

- *because when we read the cursings of ancient Israel we are in a better position to understand the contrasting words of the founder of the New Israel, and his prayers from the gibbet outside Jerusalem city wall become all the clearer: 'Father forgive them, for they know not what they do.'*

13–19 JANUARY   THE GREATNESS OF GOD

1 The great God; God the King of glory   *Read Psalm 24*

This Psalm is most often described as an 'entrance liturgy to the Jerusalem temple'. Verses 1–22 are a hymn to God the Creator and were probably sung by a procession of worshippers as they approached the temple mount. The ancient oriental concepts of creation pictured the world as being established on the waters, conquered and controlled through the act of creation. God the Creator is also God the victor over any forces who threaten his creation or people.

When the procession reached the temple entrance the people stopped in their tracks and those outside asked, perhaps through a priest or temple prophet, the question contained in verse 3. They were answered by the door-keeper who intones the answer defining who can enter and seek the presence of God (vv. 4–6). These verses can only be a summary of the demands of true worship. A similar entrance liturgy preserved in Psalm 15:2–5 is longer and contains ten requirements. It is sometimes suggested that this reflects the tradition of the Ten Commandments, although, on the other hand, the number of demands may be purely coincidental. The requirements for true worship are morally and inwardly motivated and do not call for outward ritualistic obligations.

After receiving the correct answers, the procession, probably carrying the ark of the covenant in joyful celebration, is given permission to enter the temple itself.

In verses 7–10, the temple gates are personified and called upon to lift up their heads to allow 'the king of glory' to enter in triumph. Another question is intoned from within asking for further identification as not everyone was allowed automatic entry. After the reply 'The Lord of Hosts', the gates are opened and the procession enters for true worship of God as king of creation and king of all glory.

2 A great deliverer; faith facing facts   *Read Psalm 75*

This Psalm has been labelled a thanksgiving of the community and contains a prophetic oracle in verses 2–5 uttered by a prophet in God's name. The Psalm is best understood as liturgical dialogue.

It is obvious from the opening verse that the congregation is giving voice to its thanksgiving for a recent action of deliverance on their behalf by God.

In verses 2–5 God responds to this thanksgiving through one of the temple prophets. God is sovereign over all human deeds and over the physical world. This is no sentimental word; the boastful and the wicked are warned against using their self-reliance in any form of arrogance in verses 4–5.

God is all-powerful and no force from any direction is able to alter his judgments. These will be administered by God himself and are symbolized by a cup of foaming wine which the wicked will drain 'to the dregs' ensuring their own destruction.

A different note is sounded in verses 9–10 for the singer, full of hope, is able to thank God and offer praise. The confidence for this thanksgiving lies in God as the dispenser of justice who will exalt the righteous and humble the wicked.

3   A great refuge; in God's own city   *Read Psalm 46*

This Psalm consists of three sections and it is generally believed that the refrain or chorus of verses 7 and 11 should also appear after verse 3.

The first section proclaims hope and confidence in God's providence even in the midst of the worst chaotic conditions imaginable. God has shown his sovereign power through his creative acts at the very beginning (Genesis 1) and thus the threats of chaos to engulf the world again (v. 3) do not make the worshipper afraid.

The second section describes Zion as God's city and its citizens will enjoy his protection. No river ran through Jerusalem and even the Gihon spring lay outside the eastern wall. The reference in the Psalm is to the river flowing from paradise (Genesis 2:10) with its life-giving blessings. God's presence in the midst of his city brought security to its people. The chorus of verse 7 shows the confidence of the citizens as God is with them. The same theme is expressed in Isaiah 7:14.

The last section declares the citizens' sure hope for the future when God will establish anew a period of universal peace (see Isaiah 2:4ff; Micah 4:1ff).

The Psalm closes once again with its refrain of absolute assurance (v. 11).

4   A great name; the exalted Lord   *Read Psalm 113*

Psalm 113 stands at the head of a collection of Psalms known in Judaism as the Hallel (Psalms 113–118), a name taken from 'Hallelujah' which is the first word of every Psalm in this collection and is translated usually as 'Praise the Lord'. Psalm 113 is a hymn praising the name of the Lord. God is seen as great and supreme over the whole of creation yet is humble enough to understand and come to meet the needs of his special people.

The opening call to praise (vv. 1–4) was perhaps sung by a soloist but pivots on the 'name of the Lord' which is uttered three times in the first three verses. The name of God is a reference to the revelation of his character. The universal sway of God's greatness is emphasized both by reference to time, 'now and evermore', and also by its geographical extent, 'from the rising of the sun to its setting', the ancient oriental way of referring to east and west.

The second portion of the Psalm announces that God's greatness is incomparable. The phrase 'our God' is a subtle way of suggesting that it is only his own covenant people who really know his mystery. The mighty transcendent God is willing to stoop to help his own people in trouble and tribulation. This is a third dimension of his greatness, the first two of time and space having already been praised in the opening verses. That God deigns to look (vv. 5–6) means that he is willing to act on behalf of the needy. The weak and the poor will be especially helped by him. The fact that God elevates the humble from the 'rubbish heap', the lowliest position possible, to the status of 'princes' and brings happiness to the 'women of a childless house', who were much despised in oriental culture, is a true mark of his greatness. Many interpreters have pointed out that verses 7–9 are almost a word-for-word quotation from the Song of Hannah in 1 Samuel 2:8. Throughout the second half of this Psalm the worshippers declare the greatness of their God who is so mighty and yet is willing to show a practical concern for the lowly and needy. This is true preparation for the Gospel and for the Son of God who will come in time and be humbled, as the hymn preserved by Paul in Philippians 2:5–11 reminds us.

5 A great preserver; an unsearchable God   *Read Psalm 145*

Two of the most important characteristics of the hymn of praise are to be discerned in Psalm 145, namely, offering praise for God's greatness and calling on others to come and join in this praise. Praise for God's greatness permeates this Psalm and is accompanied by interjections for others to participate in this action of praise. Every invitation is followed by another description of God's mighty works (vv. 3, 8–9, 13–20).

The Psalm opens with a soloist leading the congregation in praise

(vv. 1–2) but by the end all people on earth will praise God's name (v. 21). The Psalm is acrostic in structure, thus every verse begins with a consecutive letter of the Hebrew alphabet. This structure probably indicates that the Psalm was a later addition to Israel's hymnology. The Psalm's main note of praise is sounded from its very beginning (vv. 1–3) when a soloist utters unmistakably that the Psalm is intended to praise God as king of the whole universe.

It is impossible not to be aware of God's praise, for one generation proclaims his greatness to the next (vv. 4–7) and praise becomes part of the whole way of life which would be empty and meaningless without it. In this section God's mighty acts as Creator and Redeemer have been woven together until they are almost inseparable.

Verses 8–9 praise God because of his compassionate character and the adjectives are completely different from those used in the previous sections. His true greatness is reflected in his grace and compassion. Many have suggested that it was intended that a larger choir sing this section.

Verses 10–20 form a general hymn of thanksgiving proclaiming confidently God's splendour and majesty. The word 'kingdom' as used in verse 13 does not refer to any geographical area but to his reign and sovereignty. The verses are a catalogue of God's faithfulness to his promises and his gracious acts. Yet, there is a stern note of warning in verse 20 that he will destroy the wicked.

The Psalm closes with the note on which it opened, reaching a climax in verse 21 where the praise of the soloist now becomes part of the praise of all the people. This repetition is deliberate, for the primary motive is to invite all people to join in this praise to the great God.

6 A great manifestation: God's presence   *Read Psalm 29*

The main thrust of this Psalm is the manifestation of God's presence through the thunderstorm. Some commentators see the Psalm as a hymn composed especially for use at the beginning of the season of the autumn rains. There is a very close association between God and the thunderstorm in the Old Testament. Many interpreters see here a strong connection between this Psalm and an ancient Canaanite hymn to Baal-Hadad, the god of weather. If there was any borrowing, then the hymn has been well and truly immersed in Israelite theology and declares Yahweh's unquestionable authority.

Psalm 29 opens with a call to worship God (vv. 1–2) but this time even the heavenly powers are commanded to join in the worshipping community and to acknowledge God as king. Israel's neighbours worshipped many gods but Israel knew only one God. Sometimes this is articulated as if Yahweh were the chief of the gods. This thought does not cast doubts on Yahweh's uniqueness but confirms that any other heavenly beings are part of the heavenly court and are all subject to God's will. These are servants of God and worship him in the heavenly temple as the congregation should do on earth (see Hebrews 8:1–7).

Verses 3–9 describe God's epiphany on earth through the voice of the thunder. The phrase 'the voice of the Lord' appears seven times suggesting the continuous ferocity of the thunderstorm when there is no respite. The whole picture is one of God's awesome majesty and the terrible effects of this particular storm, probably personally experienced by the poet, are described. This is obviously no local storm but a great manifestation of the glory of God extending from creation ('over the waters'); his work in history ('the wilderness of Kadesh') which reminds us of Moses; and over the whole known world from Lebanon in the north to Kadesh in the south, including the desert areas, mountains and seas. There is only one possible response and that is a shout of 'Glory' (verse 9).

The Psalm closes with a thankful note. Babylon's greatest fear was flooding and she began her New Year celebrations when the rains stopped. She knew then that the rivers would subside and the fields could be planted. Israel's greatest fear was the desert and drought, and once the autumn thunderstorm heralded the onslaught of the coming rains she knew that her next spring would be fruitful indeed. This is why Israel celebrates her New Year in the autumn. The storm is a sign of God's glory but is also a sign of his blessing. This true blessing is crystallized in the word 'peace' which includes not just the absence of war but the whole well-being of God's people.

GUIDELINES

It is important to remember God's greatness in all manner of ways and this is what the temple congregation was able to accomplish through these Psalms. When people take the centre, God is pushed aside and marginalized. The word 'worship' is derived from 'worthship' and that means recognizing God in his greatness for all that he is worth. Let us think again about God's greatness, so that our God might not be—as in the title of J.B. Phillips' book—too small.

Let us pray for those who see God as no more than a 'little mascot' for their religion rather than as the almighty Creator-King.

Let us pray for those who cannot accept God's majesty.

Let us ask that we be given grace and vision to appreciate God as he really is.

The Acts of the Apostles 1—12

The author

There are four intriguing passages in Acts where the author seems to have been involved in the action. He joins the expedition from Troas to Macedonia (16:10–17); he appears to stay in Philippi until Paul's return there 20:6, but accompanies him to Jerusalem (20:6–15; 21:1–18), and on to Rome (27:1—28:16). Most scholars would accept the tradition that this companion/author was Luke, mentioned three times in the New Testament (Colossians 4:14; Philemon 24; 2 Timothy 4:11). He is probably the only non-Jewish writer in the New Testament, and how he first heard the gospel we do not know. His two-volume work Luke–Acts is dedicated to a Theophilus, who perhaps sponsored it.

The book

My earliest memories of Acts are of drawing boring maps at school of the journeys of St Paul. I did not register why he went on these journeys! So, what is the book all about?

It does provide a useful backcloth. It is fascinating to see how Paul's letters fit (or don't fit) into the course of his activities in Acts.

It paints a vivid picture of the earliest days of the Christian church. Even if the book was written some considerable time later (and scholars disagree on this) there are plenty of clues that the Church it describes was the primitive one. Luke was a reputable historian—he'd read the documents, interviewed witnesses and endeavoured to produce an 'orderly' account (Luke 1:1–4) in the context of contemporary history (Luke 2:1–3, Acts 18:1–2).

It studies the contributions of early Christian workers, notably Peter and Paul, but does not give their biographies. Peter 'disappears' after chapter 15, and the end of the book leaves Paul's future hanging in the air. Other characters, too, claim our interest.

It is selective history, with at least two messages.

First, Luke and Acts together describe a journey: Luke—the journey of Jesus to Jerusalem to die and rise again, to make possible God's plan of salvation for the world, 'a light for revelation to the Gentiles' (Luke 2:32); Acts—a journey of that good news to 'the ends of the earth' (Acts 1:8), although in fact the end of the book is not the end of the task. We go as far as Rome and Paul preaching the kingdom of God 'boldly and without hindrance' (Acts 28:31).

Secondly, and most importantly, however, the main character who initiates and directs every movement is God in Jesus through the Holy Spirit. The gospel told how Jesus *began* his work (Acts 1:1). Acts tells us how the exalted Jesus *continues* the work through his Spirit in his followers.

The challenges for us

* *to try to get to grips with the history of Christianity. It will 'anchor' our faith (Luke 1:4).*

* *to be positive about the world in which we live. God is at work in it and is changing it.*

* *to believe that the Spirit of Jesus is in us, to continue his work of witness and mighty deeds.*

The notes are based on the New International Version of the Bible.

20–26 JANUARY   ACTS 1:1—5:42

1   Waiting for the Spirit   *Read Acts 1:1–26*

If you want a message remembered, repeat it (*ad nauseam*, according to commercial television). Luke knew this principle. Later in Acts he relates the conversion of Saul three times and the story of Cornelius twice. So here, the first and second volumes are tied firmly together and important events are repeated.

The interim period—important lessons taught
Jesus showed that he was truly alive again (Luke 24:37–43; v. 3), and used 'convincing proofs' (it is hard to get super-spiritual about boiled fish!).

Jesus ordered them to *wait*. The Spirit would come to them and in the Spirit's power they would spread the gospel in ever-widening circles (Luke 24:47–49; vv. 4, 8). Each week of these readings will represent movement: week 1—Jerusalem, week 2—Judea and Samaria, week 3—(and the rest of Acts)—the 'ends of the earth'.

Jesus returned to his Father and, before the Spirit could come, they had to see him go (Luke 24:50–53; vv. 9–11). The ascension is the other half of the resurrection. They belong together. Jesus is raised—'exalted' (2:32–33). It means that Jesus is in a position of glory, authority and power (7:55).

Pictures of Jesus sitting on a cloud, or his feet dangling in the air, have not helped people to accept the historicity of the ascension. But 'if the spectators say they saw a short vertical movement and then a vague luminosity—and then nothing—have we any reason to object?' (C.S. Lewis, *Miracles*).

So the community waited, but 'waiting' in the Bible means more than hanging around aimlessly. They prayed hard (v. 14).

The interim period—the Spirit conspicuously absent
In spite of Jesus' commission (and example in his lifetime), the believers were strictly Jewish-minded.

- *They hoped for a kingdom of Israel (v. 6).*

- *They observed Jewish structures (v. 15)—120 men were needed by law for a Jewish community.*

- *They thought in Jewish concepts. There had still to be 12 apostles (standing for the 12 tribes of Israel). Commentators differ about whether this act was justified.*

Their reliance on these structures is not surprising. Only God's Spirit can work radical changes.

2   The Holy Spirit comes   *Read Acts 2:1–13*

What did it mean?
This was the beginning of the end times. In verse 17 Peter points out that God had promised to 'pour out his Spirit *in the last days*'.

The Church was born. Just as the Holy Spirit's presence and power surrounded the birth of Jesus (Luke 1:35 etc), so here the birth of his Church is the work of the Spirit. Pentecost was appropriate, the 'feast of weeks' when the firstfruits of the wheat harvest were offered (Exodus 23:16; Leviticus 23:15–21).

The Church was equipped for the task of being witnesses, just as

Jesus himself had been equipped (Luke 3:22; 4:14).

Good news for the world is symbolized, as people 'from every nation' (v. 5) hear their own language (v. 6, 8, 11): symbolic, however, because the crowds consisted of Jews and converts, rather than Gentiles. Pentecost could be significant here too, as it also celebrated God's giving of the law on Sinai and one rabbinic tradition taught that 'every nation received the law in their own language'.

Did it reverse the curse of Babel (Genesis 11:9)? It is not clear whether or not this was in Luke's mind.

What actually happened?

It is difficult to say, since supernatural events in the Bible use symbolic language. There was a sound *like* a wind, and an appearance *like* tongues of fire, and if they were all babbling strange words at once, how could individuals literally hear a message for them? A miracle is being described.

The whole group of believers (about 120, 1:15) were probably in a large room. Suddenly the Spirit came and strange words of praise burst from them all. They rushed into the street, still loudly praising God. But what about the foreign languages heard? They weren't necessary. Peter goes on to preach the gospel, presumably in Aramaic, and was perfectly intelligible. Probably we have here the same phenomenon as in 1 Corinthians 14, but snippets of foreign phrases were heard which amazed the crowd and captured their attention.

'Rushing wind' is particularly apt. In both Hebrew and Greek the same word is used for 'wind', 'spirit' and 'breath'. God breathed new life into the waiting Church, just as in John's Gospel Jesus 'breathed' the Spirit into his disciples (John 20:22).

3   The Spirit enables witnessing   *Read Acts 2:1–41*

After the Spirit came upon Jesus, his ministry assumed a fourfold pattern: he taught (Luke 4:18f.), he did mighty works (Luke 4:31f.), he called people to follow (Luke 5:1f.), and he faced opposition (Luke 5:17f.). With the coming of the Spirit on the believers, it is no surprise to find the same pattern (see 2:14f., 3:1f., 2:40f., 4:1f.).

The argument of Peter's sermon is complicated but this is the gist:

'You are seeing the gift which God promised, poured out through Jesus. Jesus is God's Messiah, but also has the authority of God himself [*Lord, at his right hand*]. Repent and believe this and, with forgiveness, you too will receive the gift of the Spirit.'

There are three main points:

First, this fulfils Joel 2:28–32. Clearly for Luke the fulfilment began at Jesus' birth, with visions and 'sons and daughters prophesying' (Luke 1 and 2). Whereas previously the Spirit only came upon prophets and rulers, now he is available to all.

Secondly, Jesus is God's Messiah ('anointed' one, king) raised to life by him. How do we know this?

• *Scripture foretold it. David in Psalm 16 must have been speaking of the Messiah.*

• *We have seen Jesus alive.*

Thirdly, Jesus is Lord, seated at the right hand of God. How do we know?

• *We (and you) have seen the outpouring of the Spirit.*

• *Scripture foretold it. David in Psalm 110 speaks of the Messiah being invited to share God's throne.*

Some scholars have thought that the speeches in Acts are Luke's own invention: they are similar whether it is Peter or Paul who speaks, and betray his theology. But it is reasonable that emphasis, for the Jews, is on Jesus as Messiah; there is actually great variety according to circumstances; and later the approach is different for the Gentiles.

Peter's use of scripture may seem odd to us. The Jews had their own methods of interpretation and Davidic Psalms were used messianically. Jews and Christians collected verses which were seen to have messianic significance. Psalm 110 was a favourite and was used by Jesus himself (Mark 12:35–37).

4 The Spirit-filled Church   *Read Acts 2:41–47; 4:32–5:16*

Two things characterized the new Church, which should be true of every Spirit-filled Christian community.

Growth

No doubt many of the 3,000 shortly dispersed home, but new disciples were made every day (2:47). Jerusalem was still the centre but the reports brought people in from surrounding areas (5:16), and even Jewish priests believed (6:7). Initially Luke calls them 'believers' (2:44; 4:32), but by 5:11 they have such a cohesive identity that the word 'church' (congregation) is used.

What drew them? Pre-eminently God himself (2:39, 47), but there were three channels:

- *the powerful proclamation of the apostles (4:33, 5:42).*

- *the confirmation of that message by 'signs and wonders' (2:43, 5:12).*

- *the sheer attractiveness of the community (2:47; 4:33). 'Favour' is 'grace', a reflection of the 'grace' in Jesus (Luke 2:52).*

Acts 5:13–14 is paradoxical but may indicate that only serious believers joined after the display of God's judgment.

Togetherness

There are three references to this in 2:42–47, though the Greek has different words. (See also 4:32 and 5:12.)

They were 'together' in regular meeting. They still kept the Jewish hours of prayer (3:1), attending the temple when the morning and evening sacrifice and incense were offered. But they also met in homes. 'Breaking of bread' probably describes a fellowship meal, combined with the Last Supper ritual (cf 20:7f.).

They were 'together' in sharing. Some have envisaged these early believers selling up and living together. It is more likely that they regarded their possessions as not their own, but voluntarily sold things as they saw people had need.

All, however, was not sweetness and light. Alongside the exemplary deed of Barnabas, we have Ananias and Sapphira, who, to win approval, *pretended* to present all the proceeds from property. Many have doubted the story's historicity, but it makes these points:

- *that one of the gifts of the Spirit was supernatural insight;*

- *that the spirit of evil (v. 3) was still at work against the Spirit of God (7:51; 8:18–19; 13:10–11);*

- *that at this precarious stage in the Church's life, putting God to the test (5:9) earned summary divine judgment. Did Luke have in mind the sin of Achan in Joshua 7?*

5 The power of Jesus' name   *Read Acts 3:1–26*

'All hail the power of Jesus' name.' It was only yesterday that a friend of mine encountered a young man physically distressed and hallucinating and spoke over him the name of Jesus. The calming effect was miraculous. In Acts, Luke attributes the same power to the 'name' as to the Spirit.

In Acts 2:38, baptism is 'in', 'on' or 'into' Jesus' name—that is, when a person calls on Jesus (22:16), or confesses his or her allegiance to Jesus saying 'Jesus is Lord' (Romans 10:9).

Miracles are performed 'in his name'—that is, with Jesus' authority, on Jesus' behalf and when there is faith in Jesus (3:16; 9:34). 'Name' means 'power' in 4:7. But it is not a magic formula. The name had no power in the hands of unbelievers (19:13–16).

The name of Jesus comes to stand for his saving, forgiving work, (4:12; 8:12; cf Matthew 1:21: Jesus means 'God saves'). The apostles suffered 'disgrace for the name' (5:41; 9:6).

At this early stage in the Church's life it is unlikely that the apostles had worked out all the implications of the way they spoke of Jesus, but Luke reflects later theology. In 2:21 Peter says that according to Joel there is salvation for all who call on the name of *the Lord* (i.e. God—Yahweh). But in Acts Christians are those who call on *Jesus'* name (9:14).

In the Old Testament the name of the Lord stands for his sovereign authority, glory, presence and power (Zechariah 14:9; Exodus 20:7). All this is now being transferred to Jesus and his name.

In Peter's sermon of 3:12–26, the same themes are covered as in chapter 2, but in a different order, with a different language and different prophecies. Many scholars see primitive theology in the range of titles applied to Jesus: the servant (vv. 13, 26), the Holy and Righteous one, the author of life, the Christ, the prophet like Moses (cf also 5:31; Prince and Saviour).

6 The unstoppable Spirit   *Read Acts 4:1–31; 5:17–42*

This is a long but exciting portion. Before reading the comments below, make your own notes from the text, collecting together:

- *points Peter makes in his defence (4:8–12; 5:29–32). What is new in his proclamation?*

- *further references to the 'name' of Jesus.*

In the steps of the Master
'They took note that these men had been with Jesus' (4:13). As with Jesus, therefore, opposition is aroused by revolutionary teaching (the resurrection, 4:2; and note the prominence of the Sadducees in Acts, who denied resurrection: 23:6–8), and by acts of healing (4:7; 5:16–17). Acts 4:5 describes the Sanhedrin, composed of the priestly party, lay readers of the community and scribes, presided over by the high priest. Caiaphas and Annas are both mentioned in the Gospels (Matthew 26:57; John 18:13).

One imprisonment or two?
Some scholars have suggested that Luke has given two accounts of only one incident, but it is hard to see any reason for this. Perhaps a better explanation is that, according to Jewish law, where an offence was committed, a warning was first issued (4:17). If the offence was repeated, punishment was then considered (5:33). Again, there was a parallel in Jesus' experience (Mark 2:23—3:6).

Unhindered progress
Another major theme is prominent in this section. God's work through his Spirit provokes fierce opposition, but cannot be hindered. Attempts are made to stop the work (4:17; 5:18, 33). But the apostles are under the authority of Jesus' own commission (4:19–20—the Church must evangelize); scripture and experience have taught that opposition itself becomes an instrument in God's plan (4:25–28), and sometimes the Lord will directly intervene (5:18–20, 24). The rabbi Gamaliel, a leading Pharisee and renowned for piety, wisely makes the point (v. 39): 'If it is from God, you will only find yourself fighting against God.' So the result is unhindered evangelism (5:42).
Note that Gamaliel's illustrations are problematic and there is no easy solution. The only known rebel Theudas lived after Gamaliel and not before Judas the Galilean (AD6).
    As an exercise, make 4:24–30 your own prayer.

'Evangelism is not based upon an imperialist craving to dominate the world, but upon a longing to share the good news of God with a world which sorely needs hope and forgiveness. It is something which springs from the deepest feelings of love and a heartfelt desire to share something which it would be selfish and irresponsible to keep to oneself' (Alister McGrath, *The Renewal of Anglicanism*, SPCK, 1993).

Acts uses three words for 'sharing the faith': evangelizing (i.e. *good news*-ing), proclaiming and witnessing. They represent the same thing. But what is the good news? Whether we preach from a pulpit, speak at groups, teach in Sunday school, or share with a friend, Acts gives us certain guidelines.

- *Trust the Spirit within us that he can use our words.*

- *Start where people are; grasp the opportunities given to us by people's questions or perplexity (2:12; 3:10). Pray for such opportunities.*

- *Point to Jesus and what he has won for us—a restored relationship with God and a new life now by his Spirit (2:22f, 38f). Jesus preached the kingdom, the early Church preached Jesus, but if Jesus is king, there is no discrepancy (Acts 28:31).*

- *Use the Bible as our authority. First-century methods of interpretation may not be appropriate today, but it is still true that we are sharing God's message, not our own thoughts. To proclaim is to be a herald with a given word.*

- *Illustrate from our own experience: 'what we have seen and heard' (4:20). There is great power in personal testimony. At the beginning of Acts the witnesses were all those who had actually seen Jesus alive, but later the word is also applied to Stephen (22:20).*

- *Give some kind of challenge (2:38). We may not win 3,000, but a friend may be willing to come to church with us.*

Write down what you have seen and heard of the Lord recently.

1   Tensions   *Read Acts 6:1–15*

In this week's section there are hints of a worldwide mission to come: the gospel spreads to Samaria through new evangelists; a man from Ethiopia is converted; and Saul is chosen to take Jesus to the Gentiles.

As a result of past wars and conquests and the attractions of trade and commerce, the Jewish people had spread throughout the Mediterranean world in large numbers. This was known as the 'diaspora' (dispersion). At the time of Jesus there were reputedly about a million Jews in Egypt alone. In 63BC the Roman Pompey captured Jerusalem, transporting thousands of Jews to Rome for his triumphal procession. Acts 2:9–11 lists the countries from which Jewish pilgrims had come for Pentecost. In those countries Jews built synagogues for prayer and study. They had their national languages, but the common tongue through the Roman world was Greek. Most of them knew little or no Hebrew (or even Aramaic), and for their meetings the Old Testament had been translated into Greek (the Septuagint or LXX). Even the Aramaic-speaking Jews in Palestine would know some Greek. This was a great asset for the mission of the Church—there were no language barriers.

Greece dominated the Roman world, not only with its language, but also with its culture: education, philosophy, theatre, sports. In Jewish communities inevitably a tension arose between those who were happy to adopt some Greek ways (the Jews in 6:5 all have Greek names) and those who were strictly 'orthodox'.

Many dispersion Jews returned to settle in Jerusalem, e.g. Barnabas (4:36). The 'freedmen' in 6:9 may have been the descendants of Pompey's prisoners, freed because Jews were regarded as unsatisfactory slaves. (They have inconvenient religious habits!) For worship they naturally gravitated towards their own countrymen. Archaeology has confirmed that there was a Greek theatre even in Jerusalem. As Jews from both groups became Christians, it seems that old tensions were transferred. It may be that the two groups were meeting separately to worship and there was resentment that all the official leaders were Aramaic-speaking, with the suspicion of favouritism. Wisely the apostles proposed a board of seven men as administrators and their names indicate that they were all Grecian Jews.

2   More Spirit-filled leaders
Read Acts 6:1–15 (again); 7:54—8:4

The seven new leaders whom the Church chose are not called deacons. The 'deacon' verb (to serve) and the noun are both found in this passage but with a wider application: verse 1 the daily 'distribution', verse 2 to 'wait' on tables, verse 4 the 'ministry' of the word. The New Testament applies the word *diakonos* to domestic servants, magistrates, Christian preachers and Christ himself (Romans 15:8). Clearly later it became an official position in the Church (Philippians 1:1; 1 Timothy 3:8f.), but the functions are not described.

The seven men in this passage had a special duty of administration, but they were chosen for their spiritual maturity (v. 3), and at least two of them go on to exercise an apostolic ministry: Stephen (vv. 8–10) and Philip (8:5–6).

Luke seems at pains to compare Stephen with the Twelve. He is full of 'grace and power' (cf 4:33). He preaches and does wonders and signs by the power of the Spirit and he is brought before the Sanhedrin. But even more striking than this is the picture of Jesus being reproduced in Stephen. The charges at his trial matched those made against Jesus (see the following notes), false witnesses are called, the glory of God is seen on his face, the same 'blasphemy' is on his lips, he asks forgiveness for his torturers, and he hands over his spirit—not however to the Father God (Luke 23:46), but to the 'Lord Jesus'.

Stephen was the first Christian to die for his allegiance to Jesus. Perhaps this explains the wording of Stephen's vision in 7:55–56. He sees Jesus, the *suffering son of Man* (rare outside the gospels) *standing* to acknowledge him and receive him. 'Do not be afraid of those who kill the body and after that can do no more... Whoever acknowledges me before men, the Son of man will also acknowledge him before the angels of God' (Luke 12:4, 8). Stephen also proved the truth of Jesus' words, 'You will be brought before rulers for my sake. This will be your chance to tell the good news. Make up your minds beforehand not to worry how you will defend yourselves, because I will give you such words and wisdom that none of your enemies will be able to refute what you say' (Luke 21:12–15, TEV).

What follows is a Christian 'diaspora'. God uses the reaction against Stephen's group in particular, and the consequent flight, to spread the gospel out into Judea and Samaria (8:4). In addition, Saul makes his first appearance, as a fanatical opponent of the Christian cause.

3   Stephen—'You always resist the Holy Spirit'
Read Acts 7:1–53

The thoughts of this speech were clearly very important to Luke. It is one of the longest in his book, but it is puzzling at first sight. Why such a long review of history? What points are being made? Does it answer the charges against Stephen? Jesus is only mentioned in one verse (v. 52). Note first the similarities with other speeches: Paul reviews history in 13:16f; Stephen follows Peter, but more vehemently, in accusing his hearers of the murder of Jesus, (v. 52b). There is, in fact, a very important and exciting message.

Two charges were brought against Stephen, stated three times (6:11, 13, 14): Stephen was blaspheming against Moses and the Law God had given through him; he was saying that Jesus would destroy the temple and its worship, which is blasphemy against God.

Two themes are covered, interwoven, which match the above charges. We may summarize them thus.

First: 'I am not blaspheming Moses. Rather it is you who through your history have always rejected God's chosen leaders: Joseph (v. 9), Moses and the Law (v. 39), the prophets who predicted the coming Messiah and Jesus himself (v. 52). To elaborate this the speech employs the method of 'typology', describing Joseph and Moses in terms reminiscent of Jesus.

- *Joseph: with his wisdom and grace compare Luke 2:52; like Jesus he is rejected by men, yet vindicated by God.*

- *Moses: is powerful in speech and action (Luke 24:19); was unrecognized as deliverer and reconciler; performed wonders and miraculous signs; predicted a prophet like himself (Deuteronomy 18:15).*

Secondly: 'Yes, the temple will come to an end, as Jesus said, but you have misused the temple. Through your history you have rejected the true nature of God and become idol worshippers.'

The danger of the temple for the Israelites was always that they would see God as confined to one locality, which made the temple into a god in itself and therefore inviolable (see Jeremiah 7:4: 'Do not trust in deceptive words and say, "This is the Temple of the Lord, the Temple of the Lord"').

This theme is expounded in a variety of ways:

- *the true God is not confined to Jerusalem: he revealed himself in Mesopotamia; he was with his people in Egypt; Joseph's tomb is in Shechem (Samaria!); he revealed himself to Moses near Mount Sinai.*

- *the tabernacle symbolized an omnipresent God, but even in the wilderness God's people rejected worship of the true God (v. 42b). 'Did you bring me sacrifices? No, you worshipped other gods.'*

- *Solomon's temple became a source of temptation (vv. 46–50). The words may even mean that God never intended it to be built. The implication could be that God's promise to David regarding a 'house' to be built by his 'son' pointed towards the 'Son of David', Jesus, and worship centred on him, present in his temple, the Church (John 2:19–21; Matthew 12:6; 1 Peter 2:4).*

However far we take it, this speech marks the beginning of a break with the temple, and rejection of the Church by the Jews, leading to wider evangelism (13:46).

4   Philip led by the Spirit of the Lord   *Read Acts 8:5–40*

Philip, the second of the Hellenistic leaders, exercises an apostolic ministry, first among the crowds in Samaria, and then to a particular individual. In the second case Luke underlines the Spirit's involvement. The passage raises at least four questions.

Who were the Samaritans?
In 722BC the Assyrians defeated Samaria in the northern kingdom of Israel, and foreign exiles from other parts of the Assyrian empire were resettled there, while leading Israelites were deported. As time passed, Judeans in the south became increasingly hostile to the Jewish Samaritan community, judging it mixed and impure. The final breach came about 200BC. The Samaritans built their own Temple on Mount Gerizim and looked forward to a 'prophet like Moses' (the 'Restorer'

of John 4:4–9, 20–26). Relationships were particularly bad in the early first century. They were seen as heretics and therefore worse than Gentiles.

Luke knew of Jesus' sympathy for them (Luke 10:33–37; 17:11–19).

Baptized, but without the Holy Spirit?

This is very odd—a unique occurrence in the New Testament. It has been explained in different ways:

- *there was the necessity for a kind of 'episcopal' laying-on of hands. But Cornelius did not need this (10:44).*

- *becoming a Christian is a two-stage process. But 2:38 makes no such division.*

- *the Samaritans' faith was defective initially. But the text does not support this, (v. 14; contrast Acts 19:1–7).*

Perhaps the best explanation lies in the fact of the Jew-Samaritan divide. God used the apostles in this way to ensure a united Church.

Where did Simon go wrong?

This story is a salutary reminder of how vulnerable Christian leaders are. Simon's previous record betrays his longing for spiritual greatness (vv. 9–10). He embraced the new faith (v. 13), but still wanted to 'amaze people with magic' and totally misunderstood God and his gifts. Verse 24 indicates a change of heart, although later legends portray him as a continuing mischief-maker, claiming to be a Christ-figure. 'Simony' today means attempting to buy a position in the church.

Was the 'Ethiopian' a Gentile?

Luke, perhaps deliberately, does not make this clear. But the hints are there (and signal therefore a Gentile mission). The man was an important official (from 'Ethiopia'—present-day Sudan), but no eunuch could become a proselyte. Like Cornelius later, however, he was deeply devoted to the God of Israel, though barred from the temple proper. He is foreshadowed in the Old Testament (Isaiah 56:3–8).

5 Saul—'Who are you, Lord' *Read Acts 9:1–19*

'Lord' in the Bible sometimes means little more than 'Sir' (Luke 7:6), but put yourself in Saul's position. Imagine his perplexity. He had worshipped and served 'the Lord' devotedly all through his life and now, to his horror, a heavenly 'Lord' accuses him of personal assault. 'The Lord' turns out to be Jesus, and consistently so throughout this passage (vv. 13, 15, 17). Small wonder then that Saul's immediate proclamation is a little different: 'Jesus, the Son of God' (v. 20).

Although some have seen a different Paul in Acts from the Paul of the letters, this event would account for the thrust of his later teaching.

- *The 'Lord God' seems little different from the 'Lord Jesus' (Philippians 2:9–11; Colossians 1:15–19).*

- *Jesus and his followers are bound together in a close union (v. 4; cf Romans 6:3–5). They are 'in Christ'.*

- *Our spiritual rescue depends entirely on God's love and favour and owes nothing to our efforts. Our part is to accept it with gratitude and obedience (Ephesians 2:8–10; Philippians 3:8–9).*

In Acts 'there moves a current of strong personal affection and enthusiastic admiration for Paul. Paul is the author's hero; his general aim is to describe the development of the church; but his affection and interest turned to Paul—the point of view of a personal friend and disciple—jealous of Paul's honour and reputation' (W.M. Ramsey, *St Paul, Traveller and Roman Citizen*, Hodder and Stoughton, 1908). Paul's conversion is recounted three times (22:3–21; 26:4–23) and there seems to be in the book a desire to show that Paul's spiritual status, authority and experiences match those of Peter.

Note that 'Saul' was Paul's Jewish name. He had the Latin name 'Paullus' as a Roman citizen and, not surprisingly, Luke begins to use it when Paul enters a mainly Gentile environment (13:9).

6 Barnabas—'son of encouragement' *Read Acts 9:19b–31*

Can we trust Luke's version of the facts about Paul? Obviously we must give priority to what Paul himself tells us and it is therefore important to be aware of Galatians 1:11–24 and 2 Corinthians 11:31–33. The flight from Damascus is authentic (though apparently

Paul found it embarrassing—2 Corinthians 11:30). But the rest of Luke's account needs some clarification.

- *'Many days' (v. 23): three years evidently, during which he travelled and preached in Arabia, making Damascus his base.*

- *'Brought him to the apostles' (v. 27): only Peter, it seems, with whom he stayed for a fortnight.*

- *'Moved about freely' in Jerusalem (v. 28): but it appears that Paul did not attend church meetings in Judea. He worked independently, continuing Stephen's evangelistic work.*

- *Luke confirms the departure to Cilicia. Tarsus was its capital city and Paul's home town (Acts 11:25).*

The brief glimpses we have of Barnabas in Acts 1–15 present a vivid picture of a Spirit-filled man, who was generous, in touch with people, seeing the best in them, prepared to lead, but strong enough to support the leadership qualities in others. It is significant that he knew Paul's story and vouched for him (9:27); he was later sent to Antioch and recognized God at work there; he remembered Paul and enlisted his gifts (11:22–26); he wanted to give John Mark, his cousin, a second chance and was proved right (15:37–39; Colossians 4:10).

His real name was Joseph, but he was nicknamed Barnabas (4:36) in Hebrew; this means 'son of encouragement' (Greek 'son of *paraclesis*', cf the Paraclete/Counsellor/Spirit in John 14:16).

We temporarily leave Paul here. A Samaritan wing to the Church has been established. Growth continues. The stage is set for a startling new development in God's plans for the world.

GUIDELINES

A twentieth-century Saul
Though, according to my ideas at the time, I thought I had done a good deed in burning the gospel, yet my unrest of heart increased, and for two days after that I was very miserable. On the third day, when I felt I could bear it no longer, I got up at three in the morning, and after bathing, I prayed that if there was a God at all he would reveal himself to me, and show me the way of salvation, and end his unrest of my soul. I firmly made

*up my mind that, if this prayer was not answered, I would before daylight
go down to the railway, and place my head on the line before the incoming
train.*

*I remained till about half past four praying and waiting and expecting
to see Krishna or Buddha, or some other Avatar of the Hindu religion; they
appeared not, but a light was shining in the room. I opened the door to see
where it came from, but all was dark outside. I returned inside, and the
light increased in intensity and took the form of a globe of light above the
ground, and in this light there appeared, not the form I expected, but the
living Christ whom I had counted as dead. To all eternity I shall never
forget his glorious and loving face, nor the few words which he spoke: 'Why
do you persecute me? See, I have died on the cross for you and for the whole
world.' These words were burned into my heart as by lightning, and I fell
on the ground before him. My heart was filled with inexpressible joy and
peace, and my whole life was entirely changed. Then the old Sundar Singh
died and a new Sundar Singh, to serve the Living Christ, was born.*

Sadhu Sundar Singh (1904), from A.J. Appasamy,
Sadhu Sundar Singh: A Biography, *Littleworth, 1958*

3–9 FEBRUARY   ACTS 9:32—12:25

1   Peter's wider ministry   *Read Acts 9:32–43*

Here we reach a major turning point in the book and a momentous
step forward in the Church's history. God by his Spirit demonstrates
that his plan of salvation through Jesus includes non-Jews. The
Jerusalem Church accepts this and the Church in Antioch begins
Gentile evangelism. Although Paul will become the most prominent
Gentile evangelist, the change of direction centres on Peter. He is the
key character throughout this section. After 12:19 he leaves the scene,
apart from a brief appearance in chapter 15.

Philip's experiences in Samaria and elsewhere seem to have
widened the vision of the apostles (see 8:1, 25). Peter now begins to
travel. Look at a map for Lydda, Joppa and Caesarea. Along with
proclaiming the gospel, he is empowered again to do some very Jesus-
like miracles. Aeneas reminds us of the paralysed man in Luke
5:17–26, Tabitha of Jairus' daughter in Luke 8:49–56. (Mark explains

that Jesus would have said 'Talitha, koum'. Did Peter say, 'Tabitha, koum'?) Peter went to stay with Simon—a tanner, an unclean occupation. We will meet Peter's Jewish scruples in 10:14, 28, but clearly Jesus' influence was already at work.

Luke's terminology

Religious words can arouse strong emotions. It may be helpful here to draw together some of Luke's descriptions of the early Church:

- *Of becoming a Christian: 'turned [converted] to the Lord [Jesus] (9:35; in Hebrew to 'repent' is to 'turn'); 'believed in [sometimes "into"] the Lord' (9:42); 'received the word of God' (11:1); 'repentance unto life' (11:18); 'became obedient to the faith' (6:7; see further in this week's 'Guidelines').*

- *Of being a Christian: 'saints' [set apart for God's service] (9:32); 'disciples' [learners] (9:38); 'believers' (4:32); 'brothers' (9:30) [stressing the family rather than the gender element, 11:29]; 'those who belong to the Way' (9:2); 'those who call on [the] name' (9:14, 21); 'Christians' (11:25).*

2 The Jews through 'pagan' eyes   Read Acts 10:1–8

Traditional religion in the Greco-Roman world was sterile and unsatisfying. There was the state cult with its temples, priests and regular sacrifices. It gave an impression of stability and unity, but it did not ask for belief in anything. The multitude of legendary gods and goddesses were held to have indulged in such orgies of cruelty, immorality and deceit that many people were repelled. Traditional religion offered no hope, no vital contact with the supernatural and no ideals for behaviour.

Many thoughtful people turned to philosophy. Men like Plato and Aristotle had argued for one divine Being or Cause for the universe. It made rational sense. Others were attracted to the so-called 'mystery cults' (e.g. the worship of Mithras and Cybele). They offered exciting secret ceremonies and charismatic-type experiences.

Others, however, were drawn to Judaism. It was a simple faith intelligible to the ordinary person; its one Creator God had revealed himself in history and in a holy book, and wanted friendship with humanity; it had high ethical ideals and satisfying gatherings for prayer, singing, learning and discussion. Non-Jewish males were welcomed and could even 'become' Jews (proselytes) if they renounced all other religions, including Emperor worship, and—the crunch point—submitted to circumcision and the Jewish Law. Some did (Acts 2:11; 6:5) though they were still regarded as second-class citizens, not true 'sons of Abraham', and had to pray, 'O God of *your* fathers'.

Those who baulked at circumcision came as close as they could, sometimes being known as 'worshippers of God' (13:26). Cornelius and many in his household came into their category. He was known for his faithfulness to two important Jewish requirements, prayer and almsgiving. Another Roman centurion, known to Jesus, was deeply respected by the Jewish elders, because he clearly loved the Jews and had even built a synagogue for them in Capernaum (Luke 7:4). Jesus was impressed with the faith of such non-Jews (Matthew 8:10–11). The New Testament mentions favourably two other centurions (Luke 23:47; Acts 27:1–3).

Note that a centurion was an army captain with a hundred soldiers under him. Ten such divisions made up an auxiliary regiment. The auxiliaries in the Roman army policed the provinces, while the legions were the fighting force on the borders.

3 The Gentiles through Jewish eyes *Read Acts 10:9–23*

'God does not show favouritism, but accepts men from every nation who fear him and do what is right' (10:34–35); this is an amazing statement, given the Jewish belief that they were God's chosen and privileged people, and that the judgment of God would fall upon the rest of the nations.

The Jewish view of the Gentiles is complicated and certainly there were wide variations of practice throughout the Roman world. Strict Jews would not handle any goods from Gentile hands, but trading went on. Ceremonial defilement was incurred when a Jew entered a Gentile building (John 18:28), but Jews could entertain Gentiles (10:23). In the dispersion there was a strong missionary movement and missionary literature was written. 'You travel land and sea to make a single convert,' said Jesus (Matthew 23:15). In Jewish eyes the Gentiles were doomed and their only hope was to become proselytes. The rabbi Hillel said, 'Be one of the disciples of Aaron, following after peace, loving mankind and drawing them to the Law.'

All Jews, however, held in common the importance of the food laws. Gentile food was defiled and to accept Gentile hospitality rendered a person unclean. This belief was, and still is, deeply ingrained in the orthodox Jewish consciousness.

The first lesson Peter learnt was that God now declared all food clean (ceremonially, if not hygienically). Probably Peter later remembered Jesus' own words and passed them on to Mark (Mark 7:14–19). So when the invitation came, Peter could accept Gentile hospitality with a clear conscience (10:20). Further reflection no doubt taught Peter the second lesson (10:28), that no Gentile should be regarded as unclean.

The events which followed led the Church officially to welcome Gentile believers into membership (11:18), but the implications still had to be worked out and food laws continued to be a problem (15:20; Galatians 2:11–13; Romans 14). The heart is sometimes slow to applaud what the head acknowledges. Such is the residual power of prejudice.

We began with 10:34–35. God accepts all who are seeking him and his ways, but the point of the vision to Cornelius is that he still needed to hear the gospel of Jesus (11:14).

4 The Gentile Pentecost   *Read Acts 10:1—11:18*

Jesus himself had indicated that through his ministry salvation would become available to the world. He healed Gentiles, he commended their faith, prophesied their inclusion (Luke 4:24–27; Matthew 8:11), and commissioned his disciples to embark on world evangelism (Matthew 28:19).

The earliest disciples had understandably not taken this on board: unintelligible ideas are easily forgotten; the question had hardly arisen for the Church in Jerusalem and Judea; and Jesus' own tactics had been 'the Jew first' (Matthew 10:5–6).

Luke himself saw no discrepancy. He records Jesus' concern with Gentiles, but still recognizes that there needed to be a mammoth intervention by God if the Church was to change its outlook. He tells the story at length twice (with a further summary in Acts 15). He underlines how God was in charge through visions, dreams and special operations of his Spirit:

- *the Spirit directed Peter to go to Cornelius (10:19; 11:12);*

- *even before Peter could issue a challenge (would he have demanded circumcision?), he and his six companions witnessed the coming of the Spirit on Gentiles (10:44–45);*

- *the experience was comparable not to conversions on the Day of Pentecost, but to that day's events in the Upper Room and the Spirit baptism promised by John (10:47; 11:15–17; cf 1:5).*

God himself launched the Gentile mission. The Church had to accept it (10:47–48), and did so with (perhaps rather bemused) joy (11:18).

Peter's sermon here has two points of special interest. First, outside the confines of Judea more information about Jesus' ministry was required (10:37–38). Secondly, there are hints of deeper thinking about Jesus' death (10:39). 'Hanging him on a tree' is the language of Deuteronomy 21:22f, further developed in 1 Peter 2:24 and Galatians 3:10–14.

5   The Gentile mission begins   Read Acts 11:19–30

Sometimes the Lord works in his Church through special revelations and formal decisions. Such was the case in the Cornelius incident. Sometimes however he works through spontaneous movements as at Antioch. The Gentile 'revival' there came about through Hellenistic Jews scattered after Stephen's death. They were unlikely to have heard anything about Cornelius.

The apostles had accepted Gentile membership of the Church and made a wise choice in sending Barnabas to assess what was happening, but the Jerusalem Church was too conservative to take the initiative in Gentile mission. Antioch fitted the bill perfectly.

We tend to overlook Antioch but it was due to become a great theological centre in the early Church. It was the third largest city in the empire (after Rome and Alexandria), a commercial centre, had an ambitious building programme and staged its own Greek games. Archeologists have discovered mosaics which give a picture of daily life clearer than anywhere except Pompeii. It was 'a meeting point for many nationalities, a place where barriers between Jew and Gentile were very slight, so numerous were the converts to Judaism in the city, and so high the status of the Jews there—they enjoyed full citizen rights' (Michael Green, *Evangelism in the Early Church*, Hodder & Stoughton, 1970).

The record of Paul's and Barnabas' visit to Jerusalem with famine relief has become part of a very complicated historical controversy. How do these events fit Paul's reports when he later wrote to the Galatian churches (Iconium, Lystra and Derbe)? The position taken here is that Galatians 2:1–10 gives a fuller description of the visit in verse 30. (You may find it helpful to read Galatians 2:1–10). In Acts 11 no questions are raised about whether new Gentile converts should become proselytes first and be circumcised. In Galatians 2 Paul underlines that the apostles completely accepted the Gentile ministry. Clearly, however, there was a party in the Jerusalem church which agitated for circumcision. They stirred things in Antioch (Galatians 2:11–13), and later went on to cause trouble in Paul's new churches of Lystra and elsewhere: hence Paul's Galatian letter. Eventually the conflict was so bad that a council was held in Jerusalem (Acts 15:1–2).

(Note the alternative traditional view, that Paul never mentions the 'famine' visit in Galatians 2, but is there giving his version of Acts 15.)

6 The end of an era   *Read Acts 12:1–25*

This chapter gives us some clues about dating. Herod Agrippa I died in AD44 and there is good external evidence for a severe famine in Judaea in AD46. If Luke's reporting is accurate this means that Agabus' prophecy (11:28) led to preparations in Antioch over a long period and probably the journey to Jerusalem (11:30) did not happen until after the death of Herod. Luke completes the account in 12:25.

The story of Herod and Peter's miraculous release contains many interesting features, but how does this chapter fit into Luke's pattern? Chapter 13 would have followed chapter 11 very naturally. Chapter 12 is a conclusion in two ways:

First, it concludes the material about the church in Jerusalem and about Peter. Though Peter appears briefly in chapter 15, he ceases after 12 to be the central character. Some have even suggested that here his life is symbolically completed, as a mirror of the life of Jesus. He is arrested at Passover, 'faces' death, but comes to life again.

Secondly, it concludes the first half of the book and shows 'the triumphant progress of the gospel (v. 24), which is not hindered by the death of one apostle or the imprisonment of another. When the church prays, the cause of God will go forward and his enemies will come to naught, even if this does not exempt the church from suffering and martyrdom' (I.H. Marshall, *Acts*, IVP, 1980).

Three new characters appear. *John Mark* (v. 12) will go with Paul and Barnabas. He was probably the cousin of Barnabas mentioned in Colossians 4:10 and tradition attributes Mark's Gospel to him. *James* (v. 17), the brother of Jesus (Mark 6:3), soon became the leader of the church in Jerusalem (Acts 15:13; 21:18), and had the difficult task of holding together its factions.

Herod Agrippa I should not be confused with Herod the Great at Jesus' birth (Matthew 2:1), Herod Antipas during Jesus' ministry and death (Luke 3:1; 23:6f.), and Herod Agrippa II, who appears later (Acts 25:13). They were all of one family, who successively ruled different parts of Palestine under the supervision of the Romans.

GUIDELINES

Luke's primary task in writing Acts was to record what God had done. He was not concerned with theological analysis. His account of the Holy Spirit is one-sided, stressing his role in directing mission. But the consequent picture of God is true and illuminating—a God who is sovereign and not tied to one way of working. Certain patterns, however, can be discerned to help us with the following questions.

What is conversion?
Is Paul's conversion a model? No, and yes. The Bible indicates that God 'takes by the scruff of the neck' people who will carry heavy spiritual responsibilities—Moses (Exodus 3), Isaiah (Isaiah 6), Peter (Luke 5). However, certain elements in Paul's conversion are true for every Christian, whether in a gradual or sudden experience.

• *The Lord always takes the initiative with us (2:47).*

• *Conversion is a response to Jesus and promises given through him—forgiveness of sins, gift of the Holy Spirit (2:38), salvation (4:12), membership of God's family (3:25), peace with God and other people (10:36), life (11:18).*

71

- *Conversion is the response of the heart ('turning' from evil to the Lord), the mind ('accepting the word', 'believing') and the will ('obedient to the faith').*

Baptism is the outward sign of all three points above.

What is meant by 'baptism with the Holy Spirit (1:5)?

The promises given above are all fulfilled together, when a person believes. Christians do not have to wait for the gift of the Spirit. Pentecost was an exception. The Spirit was not 'available' until Jesus ascended (John 16:7).

With the Samaritans God took unusual steps at a crisis point. The Ephesians in Acts 19 had not believed in Jesus.

The expression 'baptized with the Holy Spirit' is only used in reflecting the words of John the Baptist. For the early Church the *gift* of the Spirit is promised when a person is baptized with water. 'The New Testament knows nothing of an unbaptized Christian' (Marshall). Profound experiences of God and the Spirit regularly happen to Christians. We should all covet and rejoice in them, but it is best to use other descriptions such as 'renewal of baptismal consciousness', 'understanding the gifts bestowed on us', 'a new awareness of the presence and power of the Spirit', 'release of the Spirit'.

What is meant by 'filled with the Spirit'?

Thirty-four times in Luke–Acts 'fill' words are used in connection with the Spirit. At Pentecost the initial experience is described as being 'filled with the Spirit' (2:4; cf 9:17), and thereafter Christians who are noticeably controlled by the Spirit are described as 'full' of the Spirit (e.g. Stephen in 6:3, Barnabas in 11:24). But the phrase is also used when there is a special outpouring of the Spirit, enabling people to witness boldly or speak prophetically (4:8; 4:31; 7:55; 13:9).

How was the reception of the Spirit recognized?

Clearly in Acts when people received the Spirit, it was obvious to others (8:17). How? Some people have maintained that there was always speaking in tongues (2:4; 10:46). But Luke does not say so. More often he mentions their power to speak, their commitment and their obvious joy and praise to God (2:42–47; 3:8; 4:31; 8:39; 9:20, 27).

Further reading

Michael Green, *Evangelism in the Early Church*, Hodder & Stoughton, 1970

I.H. Marshall, *Acts*, IVP, 1980

Genesis 1–11

In some ways the stories that begin the book of Genesis, and the Bible, take us on a downward spiral. Pristine creation teems with life; woman and man live in a garden of sheer delight. But all of this soon gives way to toil, strife, and bloodshed, and ultimately the God who created life brings death for sin.

Such a precipitous path from a perfect creation is not seen in other ancient Near Eastern stories of origins. More often, distrust and dissension, trickery and treachery infest the supernatural world long before humankind appears on the scene. Numerous gods jostle for position in the divine hierarchy, ready to kill or be killed to attain their goal. Given such a context, the stories of origins contained in the opening chapters of Genesis offer much greater hope than their ancient Near Eastern counterparts: humanity may plummet from a loftier height, but that 'original', created state also serves as a reminder of what human creatures can, and ought, to be.

At the same time, the first humans offer a potentially problematic model to emulate. When they take their place in the created order their first task is to 'dominate' and 'subdue' the rest of creation. This cultural imperialism is regarded by many today with suspicion, dismay, or disfavour. In some discussions of environmental issues, this divinely given mandate has given the Judaeo-Christian tradition a bad name.

Unfortunately, things do not improve as the story continues. 'Civilized society' receives a mixed press; as the human race develops, technical advances are made, crafts are refined, cities are built, the arts take shape. And yet one does not find a consistently positive attitude towards these achievements; in fact, it is difficult to ascertain just what evaluation the narrator intends to communicate. Ambiguities abound.

These notes are based on the New Revised Standard Version.

10–16 FEBRUARY   **GENESIS 1:1—4:16**

1 *Read Genesis 1:1–13*

Chaim Potok's novel of biblical scholarship and anti-semitism, *In the Beginning*, opens with the observation: 'All beginnings are hard.' The novel's narrator has learnt this from mother, father, and mentor and the narrator himself now passes this wisdom on to his own students of the Bible, 'for I touch the raw nerves of faith, the beginnings of things'. It is true, too, of the story of origins that begins the Jewish and Christian Bibles. It, too, is 'hard'. One of the difficulties many readers of the Bible face is that these words are so familiar that they no longer provide a starting point. Beginnings are still hard, but for new reasons.

Most traditions invest significant meaning in their origins. This is true not only of religions, but of just about any institution with a heritage to look back on. According to the anthropologist Ernest Gellner, even the varied reconstructions of prehistoric human society can be traced to modern political commitments. We cannot shake off the sense that how things were in the beginning provides an important indicator for how they should be today, and those responsible for formulating foundation stories seem to be aware of the freighted meanings the story possesses.

We tend to think of Genesis 1 as recording God's creating *ex nihilo*, 'from nothing'. Certainly, to begin with, God has very little to work with! But there is a dark, watery chaos, and 'creating' seems to have a lot to do with ordering. The main emphasis falls on *separations*: light from dark, watery heavens from watery deep, land from sea. It is this ordering of the cosmos that eventually allows life to take root and blossom. The 'new' things God makes for this ordered world are few: light to partner darkness, vegetation from the earth. More will follow, of course, but the emphasis is not on cosmic conjuring, but on deliberate ordering.

Yet, there are some things our author refrains from telling us. This is 'the beginning'—but along with the watery chaos, God is already there. There is no probing beyond this scenario to some yet earlier state. God is simply there, ready to provide order in chaos.

2 Read Genesis 1:14–25

Even while God's ordering of the cosmos is taking place, the modern reader is struck by a problem: God calls light into being on Day One (Genesis 1:3)—it is God's first word, and first creative act in the Bible—but it is not until Day Four that sources for this light are made. Commentators ancient and modern offer various 'solutions' to this problem—and others—in this account of creation: the light is God;

or it is non-astral light (e.g., from lightning); or the light is the afterglow of the Big Bang.

These solutions fail to notice how important light is in these verses. Already in verses 3–5 the word 'light' has been used five times. As the events of Day Four unfold, terms for 'light' are used another eight times in verses 14–18. As we have been already struck by the organizing God, so we see the importance of light. These lights have a special place in God's creation. The insistent language in this creation account is echoed in the majestic vision of Psalm 19:1–6, where the heavenly lights declare God's glory throughout creation in wordless speech. However, the very grandeur of the lights made them dangerous. Deuteronomy 4:19 warns against succumbing to the lure of the heavenly lights which have been 'allotted to all the peoples everywhere under heaven'—it is not they, but their Creator who is worthy of worship. It is likely that the author of Genesis 1 knew the attraction of Babylonian astral cults and so constructed this account at least in part out of concern for the seductive power of sun, moon, and stars. In Genesis 1, all these players take their proper role. The God who called light into being now assigns these bearers of light their proper place and function. They act at his behest; he is their Lord.

God created a wondrous world; but our author knew that these very wonders would claim service and worship rather than their Creator. Rightly understood, our reading implies, the world is seen to derive from the Creator who alone is worthy of worship.

3   Read Genesis 1:26—2:3

Up to this point, all that God had made was 'good', but none of it was like God. But on Day Six, in the afternoon—or at least, after the creation of earthly creatures to go with those of the air and sea—God makes 'mankind in our image' (1:26). This phrase, 'made in the image of God', has occasioned prolonged, probing, and profound debate over the centuries. Even if the depths of this discussion cannot be explored, our verses do at least suggest to us that being human means to be like God, and they further suggest some ways in which this might be so.

In the initial deliberation over making humans in 1:26, God identifies these particular beings with God's own place in the order of things—and order is important! The Creator is the one who controls creation; and nature reflects glory back to its maker. Over this, humankind too will exercise 'dominion'. In some way, humanity must master nature, and not allow nature to be its master.

To whom is God speaking, and with whom deliberating? Here, in this beginning, God is in community. Other living creatures are brought forth in swarms and flocks and herds. The human creatures, made in God's image, are male and female—in community. Our passage is silent about the numbers of humans created, although the language of 'male and female' seems to anticipate the first human couple whose story is related in the next chapter. Regardless of numbers, the detail of gender strongly implies the communal nature of the creature—which is to be like God.

Finally, on Day Seven—God rests (= Hebrew *shabbat* = Sabbath). Even this divine action is to be part of human pattern and experience. Exodus 20:8–11 institutes the law of sabbath rest, but the logic of the legislation is rooted firmly in divine precedent in the week of creation. This is no simple 'rest day', however, but participation in a day specially blessed by God. It is a sacred day, and perhaps to observe its divine character is also to bear the likeness of God in the world.

4 Read Genesis 2:4–25

With God's rest, the reader, too, pauses. The work of creation is finished. Something new is introduced; the words 'these are the generations of' act as the superscriptions of new sections on seven occasions in Genesis (one of these, at 5:1, has a slight variation in wording). Because there are six other occasions when the 'generations' formula serves as an introduction, we can be fairly sure it does this job in 2:4 as well.

But what should be 'new' sounds eerily familiar. We have already read of the week of creating 'the heavens and the earth', and now we're back at the day of the Lord God's making 'earth and heavens'. Is this reprise, recapitulation, or coda? It is not simple restatement: 'God' is now 'LORD God' (or, more precisely, 'Yahweh God'). And he exhibits a wider range of activity. Rather than simply speaking and being pleased—and resting—Lord God waters the earth, forms a man, breathes, plants a garden, and grows plants—all in 2:5–9! Already there is something about this that is disconcerting. Here, the man is made first, then the garden planted, then the vegetation brought forth; animals and the woman arrive even later. This varies markedly from Genesis 1 where human creation (male and female together) culminates God's creative activity.

Before the animals and the woman are made, the man is put in the garden, 'Eden', to tend and enjoy it. The prohibition from eating of the tree of knowledge of good and evil is the only restriction placed on him, but should this stipulation fail to be kept dire consequences follow. So there is the man, in the garden—alone. The Lord God sees this and declares it 'not good' (the first time in the Bible that something is 'not good'). So, as a consequence, the Lord God makes the animals, and the man identifies them. None of these made a suitable partner for the man, so a 'woman' is made from a rib of the man. From the start, then, they are quite literally 'one flesh' (2:24); the idea of man clinging to wife seems to have as much to do with this origin from a single whole as it does with the physical consummation of marriage.

5 Read Genesis 3:1–13

As chapter 2 ends, all is sweetness and light. The Lord, the man, the woman, the creatures and the garden are all one happy family. And, in particular, there is a naïve innocence about the man and woman: they were naked, and not ashamed (2:24). Whether bearing God's image or doing the Lord's work, the man and woman more than any other creature are like their Creator.

Now another character comes on the scene: the serpent, a crafty one. *The* craftiest one, in fact, and he has a cunning plan. The serpent has the Narnian quality of being a talking beast, and addresses the woman while she is on her own. He asks her about the instructions given by the Lord to Adam: what, in fact, *did* God say? Now, the woman is not in a good position to verify anything about what God said, for she didn't exist at the time of the earlier conversation. The serpent challenges the notion that breach of this commandment will result in death. Rather, claims the serpent, God knows that if the fruit is eaten, the humans (the 'you' address of the serpent to the woman in 3:4–5 is plural) will be like God. So the woman acts out of the best of motives: not only does the fruit look good, it is also desirable 'to make one wise' (3:6). She eats, and the man eats. They do not drop dead; but they cover their nakedness.

Then the Lord comes calling—literally. A crowded scene ensues.

Hebrew narrative prefers to have only two characters on stage at any one time; but here the Lord, the man, the woman, and the serpent are all present. Each respondent shares the same 'interview technique': do not answer the question asked by the interviewer. 'Did you eat?', asks the Lord. 'She gave it to me', says the man, avoiding the question, '...and I ate.' 'What did you do?', God asks the woman. 'The serpent tricked me', says the woman, avoiding the question, '...and I ate'. Then the Lord turns to speak to the serpent.

Innocence is ended.

6 *Read Genesis 3:14–24*

The serpent, who initiated this train of events back in 3:1, is not interrogated by the Lord: no more tricks allowed. Rather, God addresses the serpent directly, accepting the woman's word that the serpent did as she described. The relationship the two have struck at their first encounter is confirmed and made permanent: they shall remain enemies, and so shall their offspring.

Similarly, the relationship between woman and man is splintered. The two who came from the one source will now live in dissension and antagonism, rather than the unity that was their original lot. This aspect emerges in the 'curse' on the woman—'your desire shall be for your husband, and he shall rule over you'—wording reproduced almost precisely in the story of Cain in the next chapter (4:7). There, sin desires to master Cain; here, the woman will desire to master her husband, but he will master her. The mutuality of their former state is replaced by antagonism—or worse. Meanwhile, to the man who came from the earth (2:7) the earth will be cursed. He has lost the unity with his partner, now he damages his link to his 'source': tending the earth will now be a matter of painful struggle.

If only the Lord had not laid on the man the seemingly arbitrary prohibition against eating the fruit of that lone tree. If only he had given the instruction after making the woman rather than before. If only... So why was this discipline laid on the human couple? It seems only to have led to the reversal of all the good things that God had made. Philip Davies offers the attractive suggestion that it is precisely this stumbling block that ultimately allows fulfillment of the mandate given the human couple in 1:28, to 'fill the earth and subdue it'. How could they fulfill this mandate—their destiny—if they remained closeted up in paradise? In the terms of the story, this crime (another sense for *felix culpa*?) against God's express command impels the human couple into the world to toil by their wits.

GUIDELINES

This week's notes raise many issues. Among them, consider:

- *'You must not read things into the text!' Or so we are usually told. With the stories of Genesis, however, the reader cannot help but fill the gaps, supply motivations, reconcile discrepancies, relate events, and so on, in the effort to understand these stories which have been so imbued with meaning. We need to read both attentively and creatively.*

- *Creativity, it seems, lies at the heart of what it means to be human. In different ways in these readings, humans bear aspects of the divine. We may be unclear about what precisely God's 'image' may be, but humans have it. God and humans both tend the garden; God makes the animals while the man gives them identity; God is one, and the human couple is one. The connections between Creator and human creature are manifold.*

- *The rest of creation can be pretty special too. Although the wonders of creation are sometimes used as a 'proof' of God's existence, in the Bible these wonders can attract the devotion due to the Creator. Warnings against idolatry (as in Deuteronomy 4:17–18) attempt to safeguard the right relationship between God and nature.*

17–23 FEBRUARY   GENESIS 4:1—6:8

1 Read Genesis 4:1–16

Luther thought that once you were through Genesis 1–3, things got easier for the interpreter. There is something in this, for the first three chapters of Genesis are highly significant, as we have seen. On the other hand, the story of Cain and Abel presents many ambiguities and puzzles and one is less certain about Luther's confidence in being on firm ground!

Even the opening announcement of the births of the brothers is odd. The man (Hebrew = *'adam*) and Eve (named in 3:20) conceive a child—but why does Eve credit Yahweh with assistance for the birth? This has troubled commentators for centuries, and the Hebrew itself is no help but rather is part of the problem. The possibilities range from Eve's mistaken understanding that Yahweh is the father, through to the possibility that she is simply offering this child in dedication to Yahweh.

More puzzling than this is the story of the brothers itself. Why is Cain's offering rejected? How does Cain know that it has been rejected? What does the Lord mean in telling Cain to 'do well' (v. 7)? Why does the Hebrew Bible fail to have any words spoken by Cain to his brother Abel in v. 8? ('Let us go out into the field' is supplied by the ancient versions.) There are no fully satisfactory answers to these questions, and every reader is forced to read between the lines. Most 'hints' have been noted as long as the 'problems' themselves. For instance, is it significant that *in the course of time* (eventually?) Cain brings his offering, while Abel brings of the *firstlings*—and of that, the best bits? Without some surmise of this kind, the story makes less sense.

The fratricide is committed. The opening chapters of Genesis have something of the feel of 'crime and punishment' about them; often it is suggested that God's punishments are especially suited to the crime. But here there is no capital punishment for a life taken. Rather, Yahweh takes special care that Cain's life will be protected as he wanders in the land of Nod. Yahweh's relationship with Cain seems almost indulgent when you put this act of care alongside the counsel given in 4:6–7.

2 Read Genesis 4:17–26

As the first couple 'knew' each other and bore offspring, so too the human race grows again through the murderer, Cain, knowing his wife, although we are not told where she comes from. Through this line 'civilization' comes into being. Cain's son, Enoch, builds the first city (some unusual Hebrew grammar makes this understanding less than certain, however), and while cities enjoy something of a mixed press in Genesis, it is quite an achievement to be responsible for this fundamental social institution.

Lamech is the fifth generation from Cain, and is the Bible's first bigamist, polygamy being a marital pattern that will be found in much of the Old Testament. He has three sons and one daughter—one of the three daughters (always given in the 'sister' rather than the 'daughter' relationship) in the Genesis genealogies. Each of her brothers launches yet another aspect of culture: Jabal is a large-scale herdsman; Jubal is the patron of music; while Tubal-Cain works metal. If it is right to see Enoch as the city-builder, then Lamech and his sons parallel Cain and his son. This is only fitting, for Lamech himself corresponds to Cain, carrying on the violent part of Cain's legacy. It is important to recognize that Lamech's saying in 4:23–24 is in poetry: Lamech did not commit two murders, but only one. The 'seconding sequence' pattern that is the hallmark of Hebrew poetry might give the impression of a double homicide.

The chapter closes by reporting the birth of another son to Adam and Eve. The final remark, that at this time 'people began to call on the name of Yahweh', surprises us for two reasons. First, since Yahweh has been conversing with his human creation since the beginning, what was he called before? Or wasn't this name known to Adam, Eve, or Cain? Secondly, Exodus records in two places the giving of the name of 'Yahweh' to Moses as something *new* (Exodus 3:14–15; 6:2–3). Still, our narrator wants us to see this God as intimately connected to the growing human family, even at this early stage. There are no nations and no national gods; Yahweh is Lord of everyone.

3   Read Genesis 5:1–5

With another list of 'generations' (as in 2:4), the narrator pauses to review. This gives opportunity for a timely reminder that human creatures are those who specially bear the divine image. This is a salutary reminder, for bit by bit the image flakes away. Human society is fractured, and the wholeness of man and woman splintered, a defacement of the divine image probably furthered by Lamech's marital arrangements (4:19). The problem of gender plagues us still, and plagues our language as well. Verses 1–2 use 'adam three times for which the NRSV offers 'Adam', 'humankind' and '"Humankind"'. Translation is always a tricky business, but this arrangement obscures something that the Hebrew insists on. God created 'adam in his image, male and female, and he named them 'adam. The unity of the male/female bearing of the divine image is reasserted, even if the social context of the biblical text is strongly patriarchal.

Fathering marks much of these opening chapters, as the growth of the human family is told from an almost exclusively male perspective. The activity of fathering itself takes on an aspect of the divine in 5:3. Just as Adam was made in God's likeness, so his son, Seth (Abel's replacement, cf 4:25) is born in Adam's likeness and image. This deliberate language suggests the importance of transmission of image—but one is left wondering about how this works. Is Adam passing on at least some part of the divine image that he received? Or is it rather that Seth takes on Adam's 'template' without reference to the divine? It is difficult to decide; nor are Adam's other offspring similarly described. Since the narrator speaks of 'his' (i.e. Adam's) likeness and image, the latter seems preferable.

At this point, Adam dies; though the narrator records the first man's death, Eve's death is not noticed. Many times in the Old Testament, strong and vigorous women lose their identity in the story (the nameless mother of Samson is but one example) to a less impressive male character. One has a sense of nostalgia at the death of Adam; but the loss of the human family's mother passes without comment.

4 Read Genesis 5:21–24

Genealogies do not make inspiring reading. They lack something in plot, if nothing else. On the other hand they often contain material of considerable interest. In Genesis 5, for example, the line described bears an uncanny resemblance to that offered in the genealogy of Cain in 4:17–22. Many of the names are similar, but they come in different order and there are enough niggling differences to keep the lists distinct.

Of more immediate interest are the vignettes sometimes embedded in the genealogy. The little notice about Nimrod, the mighty hunter, in Genesis 10:8–14 is strangely evocative; there is similar relief in the lists that begin 1 Chronicles (e.g. 2:34–35; 4:9–10). But the most important of such notices must be this fleeting description of Enoch who 'walked with God; then he was no more, because God took him'. This is good Sunday School stuff, and I remember from my childhood learning that Enoch was the one who 'didn't die'. But there are other things to notice about Enoch that the narrator does not draw to our attention. Enoch's father, Jared, lives 962 years; Enoch's son, Methuselah, lived the longest of them all, dying after 969 years. But Enoch was 'taken' after only 365 years—corresponding to the number

83

of days in the solar calendar. And he is the seventh generation from Adam, a number of significance picked up in the New Testament (Jude 14–15). Clearly Enoch was a figure of great interest and importance.

What was it that made Enoch so special? What did he do to merit being 'taken' by God? Speculation runs riot in later literature. Ecclesiasticus 44:16 holds him up as a model of repentance; Hebrews 11:5 says that Enoch 'pleased' God (following the Septuagint), and thus evidenced faith. The book of *Jubilees*, which retells the stories of Genesis, takes a lively interest in Enoch, presenting him as the first to work out the calendar and as the recipient of divine secrets, this latter being most important for the apocalyptic books that were written in his name.

If Enoch is for us simply a model of superlative piety, to those of earlier times he was one who had received a revelation prior to that of Moses and, in some sense, was even closer to God than that great leader of Israel.

5   Read Genesis 5:25–32

Beginning with Adam, this genealogy ends with Noah. By this point the correspondences between this list and that of 4:17–18 are clear and so striking that it must be that they are variants of the same tradition. But especially in the figure of Lamech himself, the two lists give quite different impressions.

Noah is the tenth generation from Adam. As Enoch had special features, some explicitly noted, some implicitly, so too does Noah. He is the first figure in the genealogy to be born after Adam's death—and he will be a 'second Adam', after the destruction of the rest of the human family in the flood. The flood is anticipated in the death of Methuselah: his age of death, 969, tallies with the year the flood took place. (Lamech, Noah's father, died at age 777—again an 'interesting' number—but five years before the flood.) Although we don't get much plot in this genealogy, it seems clear that its author has an eye on the larger picture around it. Death was promised for sin by God in Genesis 2:17, and although this isn't the 'day' of the first sin, with the figure of Noah we arrive at the point where God tries again, and makes a new start.

Lamech once again has something to say (5:29; cf 4:23–24). A wordplay on Noah's name provides the 'logic' for this brief speech.

'Noah', whose name might be related to the Hebrew word for 'rest', will bring 'relief' or 'comfort' (Hebrew: *nhm*) from the toil of the ground. It may be that this looks forward to Noah the vintner (Genesis 9:20). If this Lamech still has some of the violent overtones of chapter 4, could it be that this 'relief' from toil of the cursed earth has to do with the death that Noah's flood will bring? On either reading, with the announcement of Noah's three sons, the distance from Adam to Noah is traversed, and the story of Noah and the flood awaits.

6 *Read Genesis 6:1–8*

The genealogy of chapter 5 has laid the provided hints and anticipations of the flood—but the narrator interposes one more obscure and enigmatic tale before we focus on Noah and the flood. The story of the 'angel marriages' is given no firm chronological hold in the narrative. If anything, it pushes us back for a moment to an earlier time when people 'began' to multiply. The 'sons of God' have noticed human women; it can only mean trouble.

We aren't quite prepared for the appearance of these heavenly beings. Where have they come from? Are *these* God's conversation partners when he speaks of 'Let us' and 'our' in chapters 1 and 2? They seem to have been well-placed to get what it is they want, and they want women; and they take wives of 'all that they chose' (6:2). Who was going to stop them? About the only one who can is God; so God steps in and limits human life to 120 years. This might seem an odd response to these supernatural unions with human women. In narrative terms, it looks similar to the expulsion from the garden, carried out to prevent the disobedient Adam and Eve from eating from the tree of life (3:22). Sinful creatures must not be immortal; death must come to them eventually.

Yet the report in 6:4 hardly seems damning towards these unions. These words conjure up a potent image of a valiant age. The old King James wording has even entered the language: 'There were giants in the earth in those days.' Talk of 'heroes' and 'warriors of renown' sounds more like warm nostalgia than troubled criticism.

None the less, these alliances provide the motivation for a divine assessment of the situation. So wicked does the Lord find the human family that he regrets ever having made them in the first place. Not only this—he resolves to blot them out, along with the other living creatures. The creator God turns destroyer. Does the punishment fit the crime? To modern sensibilities, the answer must be 'no'. Who is to be held responsible for these 'angel marriages'? No mortal could have prevented them, yet judgment is to be exacted on human beings, and not only humans but all sentient things, save one group: Noah and his entourage.

GUIDELINES

These perhaps less familiar bits of Genesis might seem not very helpful. But consider:

- *Some of the 'strange' stories and characters attracted sustained attention from early Jewish and Christian writers. What did they see in them that we miss? There is at least an esoteric dimension that appealed to earlier tastes: a man who does not die; marriages between heavenly beings and human women. Does this reflect an interest in 'mystery' that lies at the heart of much religious feeling?*

- *The Bible's world—whether the world of the writers, or the world they describe—is not our world. We can become so familiar with scripture that it ceases to surprise us, and loses its power to challenge and confront. In recognizing the 'alien' aspects of biblical literature, it may be that we will be able to move beyond tradition-bound readings and see new possibilities for the Bible to engage afresh the modern context.*

- *These stories cannot help but impel us to see how quickly those aspects we identified as sharing in the 'image of God' became fouled and only a very pale reflection of their original nature. Can the identification of these aspects help us to be more faithful to the purpose that God gave to human creatures?*

24 FEBRUARY–2 MARCH   GENESIS 6:9—11:9

1   *Read Genesis 6:9—7:5*

Our third encounter with the 'generation' formula introduces a very brief genealogy and a very long story. The genealogy covers only one generation, but it provides an opportunity for the narrator to explain why Noah's family escapes judgment: it is due entirely to Noah's exceptional righteousness (6:9). By contrast, his generation is marked by 'violence and corruption', a sharpening of focus on the vaguely identified inclination to evil noted in 6:5. And unlike God's earlier expression of regret (6:7), here there is only resolve. Finally, death will be meted out for sin.

The flood story inevitably confronts us with the problem of 'composite narrative'. Only one story is told; only one narrator speaks. Yet the repetitions within the story have compelled many to resort to the surmise that two sources have been rather woodenly combined. The double-vision can be disconcerting. What is Noah to do? Should he take animals in two-by-two or seven-by-seven? And how does he know which animals are 'clean' and which 'unclean' (7:2)—of this distinction we have heard nothing. But, as the single narrative stands, the command to take seven pairs of clean animals appears to be an addendum to the original command to take single pairs, and perhaps someone of Noah's exceptional piety—reiterated in 7:1—is enough to ensure that he knows a 'clean' animal when he sees one. In any case, the obedience of Noah is impressive. The detailed instructions to build a boat (detailed enough for Noah if not for us) are offered initially without rationale. But Noah fulfills 'both' sets of instructions (6:22; 7:5) in full.

Initially, the destructive side of the impending flood confronts the reader. It is sent to kill indiscriminately. As the narrative unfolds, echoes back to Genesis 1–2 begin to emerge. The listing of animal types, the notice of male and female, the description of 'mates'—each of these sets up a resonance with acts of *creation* rather than destruction. The creator God, it seems, cannot bring himself to destroy utterly.

2   Read Genesis 7:17—8:4

It took a lot of water to accomplish the flood's purpose. Even the tops of the mountains are well submerged below the flood (7:19). In this passage we see both the rise and fall of the flood tide. God gives us an impressive display of mastery over nature. Creation came into being initially by God's controlling the unruly, chaotic waters (1:2, 7, 9) and here the waters dance to his tune. The language of the 'windows of the heavens' (7:11; 8:2) which are opened and closed appears also in the Canaanite myths that have come to light this century. Whatever their gods could do, this God can do better.

These waters perform a macabre death dance. As the water swells, the roll-call is sounded of the creatures dying in its surge. The language is inclusive and insistent—this is not simply the genocide of the human family; it is omnicide. The narrator indulges no melancholy or sentimentality; it is simply so. The scenario is all the more horrifying for the narrator's lack of pity. Life submerges beneath the waves.

'Only Noah was left, and those with him': it is a lonely seascape. In a boat, crowded with refugees fleeing a relentless and hostile force, do the survivors feel lonely? Imagination recoils at the gruesome spectacle that the narrator hides from our view. Is it just possible that *God* was beginning to feel lonely? God 'remembers' Noah and those with him; perhaps it was the deafening silence which broke into God's consciousness. Having called the survivors to mind, God calls a halt to the flood. And as the waters of chaos gave way to the wind of God in the first creation (1:2), so the wind of God blows away the flood waters in this act of re-creation (8:1). Noah and his crew come to 'rest' (the verb in Hebrew resembles Noah's name) in the mountainous *region* of ancient Urartu, roughly corresponding to the area between the Black Sea and the Caspian Sea.

3 Read Genesis 8:13–22

Finally the flood subsides and the refugees can leave the boat that has been their home for more than a year and stand on dry land. New instructions are given for the survivors as they build life anew in a world washed clean. God's instructions to Noah in 8:16–17 sound familiar, as so much of the language of this story has been already. Again we hear the echoes of the original creation account as Noah—and all living creatures—are told to 'be fruitful and multiply' (1:22, 28; cf 9:1). The act of re-creation is now launched, and the process of growth begins again.

The flood brings with it complete upheaval, and the pattern of creation/re-creation points again to new beginnings. 'All beginnings are hard'; and so it is again. With this cataclysmic event, what has changed? As Noah offers his sacrifice the 'pleasing odour' rises to the appreciative Yahweh. The aroma stirs a new resolve in the heart of God: this kind of destruction shall never again take place. What reason does God offer for this resolution? '... For the inclination of the human heart is evil from youth' (8:21). This is startling. The reason the flood was sent in the first place was because of human inclination to wickedness. What in 6:5 (cf 6:12) was cause for destruction, now becomes a 'given' in God's dealings with humankind: 'that's just the way humans are, and you take them as you find them' is the impression we are given. So again: what has changed? Humans haven't. Is it possible that God has? Perhaps the sacrificial aroma—after a year of going without—has reminded God that he needs these humans after all.

Often, in ancient Near Eastern myth, the seasons fit the pattern of a dying and rising god—or vice versa. As the life of the god ebbs and flows, so nature, acting in sympathy, goes through its cycles of growth and decay. The picture is one of transience. In 8:22, this establishment of the seasons points in the other direction. In spite of the vagaries of the seasons, life will always return; the patterns of nature ensure the permanence of life on the earth.

4 Read Genesis 9:1–17

At the first creation food was provided, but it was a vegetarian-only menu (1:29–30). At re-creation, food is again provided, but now it involves killing, as the eating of meat is permitted. This development brings with it new regulations about the shedding of blood, for the blood contains 'life'. If meat is to be eaten, it shall not be eaten with the blood; but human blood is not to be shed on penalty of 'that person's' blood being shed. There is a curious double movement regarding life here. While animal life is devalued, human life is protected—but at the cost of human life! Had Cain been judged by this principle, his own life would have been forfeit, and the developments in civilization that came through his line (4:17, 22) would have been lost. This continues the steady drift away from the situation of paradise in the first garden. The initial easy relationship between humans and animals is first lost when God provides skins for the humans to wear. With humans now becoming carnivorous, the chasm grows even wider.

The doublets in the flood story persist to the end. Although Yahweh has already resolved never again to bring universal destruction (8:21), here he does so again. There are, of course, differences. In 8:21, Yahweh makes an inner resolution (known to the narrator) unexpressed to Noah. In 9:13–15, this same resolution is expressed in conversation with Noah. More importantly, the first resolution simply promises forebearance; in the latter case, the issue is put in terms of *covenant*. This is not the first time this important theological term appears, but the first occurrence is also in the Noah story. Noah's 'personal' deliverance is couched in terms of 'covenant' at 6:18. The partners are few and the implications limited. Here, however, 'covenant' occurs seven times in the course of 9:11–17, with both partners and implications broadened considerably. Although as the concept of 'covenant' develops throughout the Old Testament it takes on a bilateral shape—commitments and obligations lie on both sides of the agreement—in this case it is a unilateral arrangement. God undertakes never to wipe out life again, and he leaves a heavenly signature in the form of the rainbow—a fitting association with rain—to confirm the contract.

5 Read Genesis 9:18–28

A pattern emerges in the opening chapters of Genesis in which 'cosmic' crimes—those with universal implications—alternate with more private offences. So Adam and Eve's disobedience (universal) is followed by the murder of Abel (private). The angel marriage/flood account (universal) is now followed by the private affair of Noah and his sons and, in particular, Ham's indiscretion.

Noah is not only righteous and a 'second Adam', of sorts; he is also the first viticulturist and wine-maker (possibly hinted at already in 5:29). This pleasant innovation almost immediately reaps dire consequences. Noah soon gets drunk and Ham (the father of Canaan), sees him lying naked. We are not prepared for this action on Noah's part, for his exemplary piety and righteousness have been constantly before us up to this point. Nevertheless, when he wakes from his stupor, he is furious about what has been 'done to him'. What *has* been 'done' to him? The two other sons obviously thought something was amiss, for they very carefully cover their father as Ham did not. So was Ham simply negligent in tending to his father's needs? Or was it disrespect shown to the patriarch? Or was it the prattling to the brothers—gossip—that was his fault? Or, on a darker level, does the combination of alcohol and nakedness hint at something sexual and, in this case, deeply offensive? Readers are left to their own instincts to solve this dilemma.

Where there is a crime, there must also be a punishment. The curse comes quickly, and it is levelled at—Canaan, not Ham. There is some ambiguity in the text about who the culprit was. 'Ham' is named, but the 'youngest son' of 9:24 does not fit the middle son. Whichever it was, the result is that Canaan is cursed to slavery, not just once by curse, but twice more in the blessings on the caring sons, Shem and Japheth. This appears to be more than simply a personal consequence. Genesis 10 describes the development of nations through Noah's three sons; that 'Canaan' should be already relegated to the status of slave has political implications for the arrangements of nation-states that will some day emerge.

6 *Read Genesis 11:1–9*

We arrive at last at the final scene of 'universal' punishment meted out for human sin in Genesis. Beginning as it does with the notice of the unified human family (11:1) it sits uneasily after the Table of Nations in Genesis 10, where location, identity and language are fully developed. Genesis 11 attributes the mechanism for this development to divine judgment. The story of the tower of Babel—as it is popularly known—is a tiny gem of story-telling; it also implies a judgment on human achievement that many could find uncongenial. But first: is this really about the 'tower of Babel'? The first concern of these people is to build a secure *city* (9:4, 5, 8) of which the tower is only a part. Further, the name 'Babel' simply gives the Hebrew term in English characters. Translated, it is 'Babylon'. Rather than a story about the 'tower of Babel', we are reading a story about the 'city of Babylon'.

Perhaps this helps to explain the negative assessment given to such 'modern' values as technological advance (baked bricks) and human achievement (monumental architecture). There is also a blow struck against the human dream of universal peace. The people of this story attempt to live together in peace and security; what they fear is dispersal (11:4). But this dream is shattered by a God who must 'come down' to see what is going on at this building site. And having seen it, he doesn't like it, and breaks up the party. At least in this case, the punishment fits the 'crime' exactly: exactly what the builders fear, dispersal, is what awaits them in the end (11:8).

There are parallels to the first 'universal' judgment: the expulsion of Adam and Eve from Eden. There, the crime had something to do with gaining in wisdom and experience (3:4–6), as here an element of social advance led to the building project. Self-discovery and peaceful living both receive judgment! Perhaps Philip Davies' suggestion about the expulsion from the garden—it impelled the human couple to fulfill their purpose—applies also to this expulsion from Babylon and contributes to the same goal of subduing all the earth.

GUIDELINES

Human growth and development should be laudable aims, but in the stories of Noah and Babylon (or 'Babel') two factors provoke further thought:

- *Should we also think of God as growing and developing? We are so used to the 'philosopher's God' who is unchanging, immutable. The Old Testament sometimes depicts a God who learns and grows, as in his understanding of his human creation in the flood story, or in gauging the piety of Job (Job 1:9; 2:3). If this is true of our Creator, should it not also be true of his creatures? Is this side of God's character also worthy of praise?*

- *Human achievement can have dire consequences. Both Noah's Beaujolais Nouveau, and the architecture of Babylon provoked unexpected results. The human mandate, at the beginning, was to 'be fruitful' and subdue the earth; but this mandate should, it seems, be fulfilled with care. At times the human family needs prodding to develop; at other times, its developments need to be pursued with caution. In an age when technical advance is a matter of course, such notions might prove salutary.*

For further reading

J. Barr, *The Garden of Eden and the Hope of Immortality*, SCM Press, 1992

P.R. Davies, *Whose Bible is it Anyway?*, Sheffield Academic Press, 1995

J. Rogerson, *Genesis 1–11*, JSOT Guides, Sheffield Academic Press, 1991

G. Wenham, *Genesis 1–15*, Word Biblical Commentary, Word, 1987

The Gospel of Matthew (3)

We pick up the story once more as Jesus enters Jerusalem. Matthew slows the pace down as he spreads the course of Jesus' last week over eight chapters. Prophetic action and public teaching give way to preparation for the disciples' future, as Jesus encourages his followers in the wisdom that will sustain them through difficult times ahead.

Fundamental to this encouragement is the story of his own passion. Jesus' willingness to live by his prayer 'Father... your kingdom come, your will be done' is a powerful example to those who must endure their own time of trial. And his faithfulness even unto death proves to be effective, as God vindicates all that he has lived and died for in the victory of Easter.

Matthew shows how a new people is born through the passion and resurrection of the Son of man: rooted in Judaism and its scriptures, but embracing Gentiles too. God's new covenant creates a people animated by the spirit that flows from the heart of the Torah and breathes through his own teaching: mercy, righteousness, love and faith. This 'gospel for a new people', as Graham Stanton has called it, can only be a sign of hope in a divided world.

The notes are based on the Revised Standard Version, though they can be used alongside any translation of the Bible.

3–9 MARCH   **MATTHEW 21:1—23:39**

---

1 Prophetic actions and their consequences
Read Matthew 21:1–22

Jesus announced his intention to travel to Jerusalem in 16:21. Now at last he arrives, accompanied by crowds of Passover pilgrims. The festival, with its celebration of the release of Israel's forebears from foreign oppression, helped to keep alive popular hopes for freedom. Nationalistic feelings inevitably ran high, and the small Roman garrison overlooking the temple in Jerusalem would be on full alert. The story of Jesus' arrival takes us back to the last time we were in Jerusalem, in 2:1ff. Once more, he creates a stir in the holy city, and his appearance again fulfils the ancient scriptures. Now as then, the one who comes as Israel's messianic king is denied a royal welcome from the authorities. So what kind of figure is he?

The answer is given in the way he deliberately chooses to enter Jerusalem. A warrior king would be riding a horse, but Jesus is intent on signalling his humility and rejection of violence (see 5:5; 11:29; 5:38ff). The crowds—many of them no doubt from Galilee—can only honour him by giving him what amounted to the 'red carpet treatment' (v. 8). They acclaim him in traditional Passover-tide words drawn from Psalm 118:25–26. And by declaring him to be a Galilean prophet, they alert us to the significance of what follows.

Jesus' action in the temple reminds us of the gestures of his prophetic predecessors (e.g. Ezekiel 5). He draws on Jeremiah 7:11 to describe its corruption. Perhaps the priestly families are making a killing from what we would now call religious tourism. The temple was, of course, the principal symbol of the identity of God's chosen people. Its architecture expressed the values of separatist holiness, with its division of Gentiles, women, men and priests from one another. The blind and the lame were excluded from its altar areas (Leviticus 21:16–24). The fact that they and the children (another group with low social status) are drawn to *Jesus* in the temple courts suggests that "something greater than the temple is here" (12:6). Jesus dares to suggest that like the barren fig-tree (in Jeremiah 8:13, the fig-tree is a symbol of God's chosen people), the 'den of robbers' is under God's curse.

Like the prophets before him, Jesus must reckon with the consequences of his prophetic actions, which are the fruit of his faithfulness and loyalty (the meaning of 'faith' in verse 21). The indignation of the priests and scribes will work the same violence as Herod in 2:16—only this time it will be directed only at Jesus, and there will be no escape.

2   Answerable to whom?   *Read Matthew 21:23–46*

According to verse 23 Jesus' arrival in Jerusalem has brought a crucial issue right to the heart of the nation: who has the right to speak and act for God in Israel? The chief priests and elders were members of the Sanhedrin, the Jewish governing council to whom Rome had delegated the day-to-day rule of Jerusalem and its surrounding region. The Sanhedrin retained its privileges, and the temple continued to function, provided they kept the peace and organized the collection and payment of the imperial taxes. Despite being answerable to the emperor, these Jewish leaders believed that they derived their ultimate authority from God, which gave them the right to question Jesus as they did.

Jesus sets out to demonstrate that they are deluding themselves. Their attitude to John the Baptist shows that they are incapable of recognizing God's authority by repenting. Their answer to Jesus' question reveals that they prefer to promote their own interests rather than God's. Like the second son in the parable, they assume that to all intents and purposes they are answerable only to themselves—which is effectively a practical atheism. The coming of God's kingdom will disclose their delusion, as they see among dishonourable sinners the capacity for repentance that they so evidently lack.

The second parable underlines the dire consequences of the self-interest of these Jewish rulers. The story reflects a familiar situation in Galilee, with absentee landlords creaming off the region's wealth. But its imagery draws on Isaiah 5, where the vineyard is Israel. There is some evidence that at the time of Jesus, the vineyard was interpreted as the temple, which explains why Jesus' hearers understood the point immediately (v. 45). Comparison with Mark's version of the parable (Mark 12:1–12) suggests that Matthew has moulded it to match the story of God's dealings with Israel, through the prophets—major (the servants of verse 34) and minor (the larger group in verse 36)—and his Son Jesus (note that in verse 39 he is killed outside the vineyard, unlike Mark 12:8). But the last word does not lie with self-interest. Even the Jewish leaders can see that the tenants deserve to lose their position. And the one whom they treat with such contempt and violence is vindicated. The verses from Psalm 118:22–23 suggest that Jesus, not the temple, is crucial to the new structure that God's kingdom will build. According to verse 43 (only in Matthew) the fruitful nation held together by the rejected son will replace the doomed nation centred on the barren temple.

Practical atheism among leaders is dangerous. If they think they are answerable only to themselves, they end up worshipping their own power. When they try to preserve this at all costs, and certainly when it collapses, the sins of the leaders are also visited on their people, and the innocent as well as the guilty suffer. Yet in the case of Jesus and Israel, that suffering is not without some fruit: the new nation arises out of the old, and opens its heart to the whole world.

3 Paying the price of power *Read Matthew 22:1–22*

The parable in verses 1–14 is similar to the one in Luke 14:15–24. In both cases there is a great banquet, and some of those who are invited fail to come. This annoys the host so much that he then extends his invitation to others, who accept it. But there the similarities end. Matthew's host is a king, while Luke's is a householder. Matthew's king sends two groups of servants, but Luke's householder sends only one servant. Matthew's servants encounter indifference, rejection and violence, but Luke's hears only excuses. Luke's householder is angry, but Matthew's king vents his anger in a display of violence which far outweighs anything his servants suffer. And when he finds a guest who had not taken the trouble to prepare himself for the feast, he reveals once more the limits of his generosity. What are we to make of Matthew's parable?

It certainly interrupts the flow of the narrative (compare Mark and Luke). It also contains echoes of the previous story: again there are two groups of servants (the prophets?), and the king's violence only intensifies the householder's reaction to his tenants. Verse 7 could well be a backward glance at the destruction of Jerusalem in AD70, though its language might just as easily be drawn from accounts of Jerusalem's destruction by the Babylonians in the sixth century BC. We should beware of attributing the parable to Matthew rather than Jesus on the grounds of its judgment theme alone, though its details do sit uneasily alongside Jesus' own rejection of violence and his criticism of rulers in 20:25. While it is not impossible that Jesus told this story, or one like it, it is more likely that Matthew is responsible for its present form. He makes the point once again that the Jewish leaders' self-interest is responsible for bringing about the doom of their nation.

The Pharisees were out to destroy Jesus earlier in the gospel (12:13ff). They and the Herodians (supporters of Herod Antipas, client ruler of Galilee) do well to try to trap Jesus with the question about taxes. Perhaps they hope to drive a wedge between him and his supporters (21:46). For Jesus to agree to the payment would mean endorsing Caesar's claim over Israel, which would not go down well with many of his Galilean followers in Jerusalem. To reject the tax would risk being branded as a political subversive, and ally him with those prepared to use revolutionary violence against Rome rather than pay the tax. In the event, Jesus' evasiveness serves him well. His statement in verse 21 does not imply a separation of politics and religion. 'What belongs to God' is Israel in its entirety, politics as well as religion. Perhaps Jesus is suggesting that those who compromise themselves by accepting the benefits of Roman rule must pay the price—with their consciences as well as their money.

4 Issues concerning the power of God   *Read Matthew 22:23–46*

The Sadducees were landowning aristocrats, from whom members of the Jerusalem priesthood were drawn. The resurrection of the dead was a latecomer to Jewish belief, occurring for the first time in Daniel, which was probably not widely accepted as part of Jewish Bible in Jesus' day. The Sadducees certainly did not recognize its authority: they treated only the books of Moses (Genesis–Deuteronomy) as scripture. Their question reflects the custom of levirate marriage set out in Deuteronomy 25:5–6. Jesus draws on popular beliefs to highlight the transformation involved in the life to come. So the Sadducees' example is absurd, because it assumes an unbroken continuity between this life and the next. And, more importantly, it rests on an inadequate appreciation of the power of God. The implication of Exodus 3:6 is that God's power to confer life is undiminished by death. So what is difficult about the resurrection of the dead? It may be that the Sadducees rejected it for other reasons. It did not merely express belief in survival after death, but hope for a coming of a new order. Why should those who occupied a privileged place in the current order in Israel promote a doctrine that would undermine this?

Jesus' reply to the Pharisees again draws on those parts of the Bible whose authority no Jew would dispute (Deuteronomy 6:5; Leviticus 19:18). Love for God and neighbour were commonly thought to express the heart of Jewish belief. But as the lawyer's question in Luke 10:29 shows, it was possible to read the law of love in a restricted way, as zealous groups like the Pharisees frequently did. Early in the Gospel, Jesus showed how he interpreted the Law (5:21ff), particularly the love of neighbour (5:43ff). Love for God means living by his unlimited generosity: that too requires a profound appreciation of the power of God.

Jesus' question about the Messiah again raises the issue of God's power. He draws on a Psalm that some Jewish groups were beginning to interpret messianically, to argue that the Messiah could not be modelled on Israel's greatest king. Israel's liberation would not be a re-run of her past imperial greatness. That would require the power of God to be expressed in revolutionary or military violence and ethnic cleansing. The new world, the fruitful nation created by God's kingdom, finds no place for that kind of divine power. Jesus' teaching throughout the gospel, and his messianic entry into Jerusalem, have made this perfectly clear.

The question of Jesus' authority has been on the agenda since 21:23. He has claimed authority to speak and act for God—to challenge the guardians of Israel's institutions, to disclose the will of God in his creative interpretations of scripture, to say how Israel's liberation will and will not come. For now, the questions cease. But when they start again, it will be away from the public gaze, behind closed doors, with the scales of power tipped decisively towards Jesus' interrogators.

5 Alarm, disturbance and warning   Read Matthew 23:1–26

Jesus now delivers the last of his public discourses. He has earlier accused Pharisees and scribes from Jerusalem of using their traditions of biblical interpretation to quench the spirit of the Law (see on 15:1–20). Here he intensifies his attack on those who abuse the privilege of occupying Moses' seat as interpreters of the Law in the synagogue. Their basic hypocrisy can be seen in their duplicity; their scrupulous and burdensome version of religion, which does not sufficiently soften their hearts to enable them to help the weak; and their obsession with public opinion and social status. These run counter to the way of life commended in the Sermon on the Mount and exemplified by Jesus throughout the Gospel. The integrity of word and action; the priority of generosity and mercy; the insistence on secret rather than public, self-serving piety; the exaltation of humility over honour and status; the creation of community ordered by egalitarian principles—these constitute the spirit of Jesus' teaching and the substance of his practice, the yardstick by which any interpretation of Israel's tradition is to be judged.

The woes which begin in verse 13 provide the counterpoint to the Beatitudes in chapter 5. Where Jesus seeks to open God's kingdom to all, particularly the excluded, these hypocrites do the opposite. And even when they are missionary-minded, they corrupt those who come under their influence. Where Jesus advocates mercy and generosity, the hypocrites encourage hard-pressed people to swear oaths on parts of the temple (rather than on the temple itself—this was considered too sacred). These would act as security to moneylenders in times of financial hardship (this practice seems to lie behind verses 16–22). If we include verse 14 (omitted from many manuscripts), it may be that Jesus is addressing wealthy but greedy Pharisees. Why not give to the needy, rather than encourage financial dependence through such oaths? Where Jesus insists that the kingdom of heaven is characterized by trust in God, righteousness (the same Greek word is translated as 'justice' in verse 23) and mercy, the hypocrites lay undue emphasis on those (relatively) minor parts of the Law that can be used to separate the pious from the rest.

Jesus' strong and colourful language, full of characteristic exaggeration, is designed to alarm the complacent and disturb the self-satisfied. It comes as a serious warning to any who occupy positions of leadership in the churches, or indeed in any part of public life. And as always, Jesus asks for nothing less than he is prepared to give.

6 Criticism and its consequences   *Read Matthew 23:27–39*

The woes continue. Pharisees have been accused of blindness in 15:14, where Jesus criticized their purity regulations. There, as here, external cleansing is not enough if greed and extortion are to be wiped out. The comparison with whitewashed tombs is a particularly powerful metaphor for hypocrisy. Tombs were painted white to warn people of their power to convey ritual contamination (according to Numbers 19, contact with the dead required seven days of purification before one could enter the temple). Verse 30 suggests that hypocrisy is fed by delusion, when people fail to see themselves in the traditional stories that have shaped their experiences. Jesus prefers to believe that for these Pharisees, it is a case of 'like father, like son', as one generation poisons another.

Verse 34 draws on 2 Chronicles 36:15–16: it is worth comparing this with Luke's version (Luke 11:49). There, Jesus refers to a saying of 'the Wisdom of God'; here he speaks as Wisdom's mouthpiece (as in 11:28–30), which underlines the authority of his words. By reminding his hearers of the fate of God's messengers, Jesus demonstrates the courage of his convictions. It is one thing to accuse others of hypocrisy in the belief that he is speaking with God's authority; it is another to live with the violent consequences of his own words, which he is clearly prepared to do. If the blood of past generations is to fall on the present, it will not leave Jesus unstained (Abel in Genesis 4:8 and Zechariah in 2 Chronicles 24:22 are the first and last martyrs in the Jewish scriptures).

It is fitting to end the final discourse on a note of tenderness. Verse 37 helps us to see the tragic dimensions of this chapter, and removes any trace of vindictiveness that a careless reading might leave, either on the part of Jesus or Matthew. Despite the best efforts of the prophets and Jesus, Jerusalem's turbulent and violent history will repeat itself (cf Jeremiah 22:5). Verse 39 marks Jesus' withdrawal from public life—until his crucifixion.

GUIDELINES

As we reach the end of the harshest of Jesus' discourses, it is worth reminding ourselves of the risks of reading Matthew's Gospel. Living as we do at a distance from the actual circumstances, both of Jesus' ministry and the church(es) for whom he was writing, can lead to a cruel caricaturing of Jewish religious teachers. Not all Pharisees and their scribes were guilty of hypocrisy. Indeed, there is evidence of contemporary Jewish teachers who were just as strong in their condemnation of hypocrisy and the power of wealth, just as insistent on the virtue of humility, and just as keen to promote an egalitarian ethos as was Jesus. So we must read with care, always alert to the fact that these words are addressed to particular opponents of Jesus and their successors in Matthew's day—and in our own, whatever our religious affiliation.

10–16 MARCH   MATTHEW 24:1—25:46

1   A call to costly endurance   *Read Matthew 24:1–14*

Jesus' remark in verse 2 picks up the earlier statements in 21:19, 22:7 and 23:38, and makes the significance of his prophetic action in 21:12 clear. Then in deed, now in word Jesus announces the destruction of the temple, not its cleansing. He speaks about the events leading up to this catastrophe in what is often called the 'Little Apocalypse'. Similar material is found in Jewish and Christian writings of this period, including Daniel 7–12 and Revelation. At first glance apocalyptic writings appear to predict the future, but much of their language is drawn from the Jewish scriptures—there are frequent allusions to the plagues of Egypt and the vivid imagery of the prophets. As we shall see, the main aim of this apocalypse, in common with the others, is to reassure the community of faith and encourage it to persevere in the face of persecution and severe distress.

Matthew's version is clearly based on Mark 13, but like Luke's account (Luke 21), there are some significant differences. Matthew's most important change lies in his understanding of the outcome of the historical process that Jesus outlines. Verse 3 should be compared with Mark 13:4 and Luke 21:7. Matthew adds the question about 'the sign of your coming and... the close of the age'. As we read further we shall see that Matthew's 'Little Apocalypse' culminates in the coming of the Son of man from heaven as judge and saviour—what Christians often call 'the Second Coming'.

Political upheaval was a regular feature of the history of the Middle East. Jesus envisages further instability, particularly as his vision of what it means to live as God's chosen people is ignored. Holiness understood as separation can only be sustained by violence—if not physical, then certainly psychological, emotional and spiritual. His alternative vision of God, messiahship and human community may lose its appeal as the tide of oppression and violence rises. The people of faith may find themselves drawn to self-styled messiahs and prophets whose agendas are more in tune with the spirit of the age. Hence the concern expressed in verse 4, repeated in verses 11 and 24: the positive aspect of not being led astray is endurance (v. 13), that is, resisting the pressure to abandon faith, to allow community life to disintegrate, and to turn inwards (vv. 10–12).

Verse 9 suggests that those who keep faith with the vision of Jesus—one which embraces the whole world, according to verse 14—will share his fate (cf 16:24ff). In the more tolerant societies of the West, this is hard to imagine. But we should never forget that when Christians, and people of any religious persuasion, take a stand against oppression and violence, as Jesus did, they run the risk of drawing what they oppose into themselves. They can only hope and pray that as they persevere, their courage will eventually give birth to a new world (v. 8).

2   A call to avoid misplaced confidence   *Read Matthew 24:15–31*

According to the Jewish historian Josephus, Jesus' contemporaries held that Daniel was a prophet for their own time. The book's stories and visions were originally compiled to sustain the faith of an earlier generation of Jews, in the aftermath of the assault of Antiochus Epiphanes and his armies on their land and temple. It was he, the 'fourth beast' in the vision of Daniel 7:23, who desecrated the temple in 167BC by erecting a statue of Zeus Olympius—the 'desolating sacrilege' of verse 15 (cf Daniel 9:27, 11:31 and 12:11; 1 Maccabees 1:54). The stories of Daniel are of course set in the sixth century BC, following the earlier destruction of the temple in 587BC by the Babylonian king Nebuchadnezzar. Jesus senses that Jerusalem will soon endure yet another onslaught from Gentile armies, this time from imperial Rome. Faced by even greater tribulation than under Nebuchadnezzar or Antiochus Epiphanes, the inhabitants of Judea will have to flee for their lives.

Verses 23–26 repeat and intensify verses 5 and 11 (vv. 25ff are not in Mark), and testify to the intense pressure on the community of faith to betray its fundamental ideals and values. False Christs and prophets would offer alternative visions of Israel's liberation and the way to achieve it. These would be based on an entirely different understanding of God's power from the one held by Jesus. He was sufficiently wise to recognize that a beleaguered people would find these alternatives attractive, especially if they offered immediate solutions based on clear strategies. Jesus promises that, despite appearances to the contrary, the sovereignty of *his* God will not be lost amidst the coming confusion and violence (v. 22). His followers are to resist the lure of alternative leaders, confident that they will recognize the true Messiah from heaven, the Son of man, when he finally comes to gather his people to himself. Verses 29–31 draw on several passages from the prophets to set out the unmistakably cosmic impact of his coming as judge and saviour: there will be no mistaking it.

Both Matthew and Mark are dependent on the vision of the appearance of 'one like a son of man' before the Ancient of Days in Daniel 7:13ff. But whereas it is possible to interpret Mark 13:24ff in terms of the Son of man's *coming to heaven before God* (which is the language of divine vindication), Matthew suggests more of a *coming from heaven to earth*. Mark may be closer to the actual teaching of Jesus, while Matthew may be casting a glance towards the beliefs of some Jewish groups about a heavenly 'Son of man', sometimes identified with the patriarch Enoch, whom they expected to appear on earth as the agent of God's judgment and salvation. Matthew insists that what they believe about *that* 'Son of man' is actually fulfilled in Jesus. Alternative ideas about the way God establishes his salvation are misguided; rival messiahs and prophets can only be false. So whatever distress and tribulation the community of faith may have to endure, they can rest assured that their confidence in the Messiah *Jesus* is never misplaced.

3 A call to vigilance   *Read Matthew 24:32–44*

Jesus has insisted that his followers stand firm in the face of upheaval and distress, but what will encourage them to do this? First Jesus assures them that they won't have to wait long for the Son of man to come: it is as if the leaves are already out on the fig trees to anticipate the arrival of summer. Then, having reminded them of God's sovereignty in verse 22, he asks them to put their trust in his own words. Verse 35 is a Semitic expression: in Jewish belief, heaven and earth will never pass away (cf 5:18), so Jesus is as good as saying, 'It is more likely that the impossible will happen than it is for my words to pass away'. As the tribulation intensifies, Jesus' followers can be confident that the Son of man will come soon.

But there is an element of ignorance about the precise timing of his coming which makes it necessary for them to be vigilant. Three times in these verses we are told about those who do not know (vv. 36, 39, 42). The first is found in Mark, though not in Luke: in view of its admission of his ignorance, it is likely to be a genuine saying of Jesus. Like him, his disciples must put their confidence in the Father. In verses 37–41, Matthew includes material found in Luke, but not in Mark, to underline the suddenness of the coming of the Son of man. Its unexpected and dramatic quality will shatter the popular 'business as usual' approach. But the disciples must not slacken their alertness for one moment, as the comparison between the Son of man and the night-time burglar shows. The parables which Matthew adds to the end of the 'Little Apocalypse' show what form this alertness is to take.

Jesus' words about the imminence of the Son of man's coming

have always been a puzzle to readers of the Gospels. A literal interpretation has encouraged an essentially world-denying faith, whose commitment to the life of the wider world has sometimes been little more than the desire to calculate its end. For some, the fact that Jesus' words were not fulfilled undermines their authority, and even makes the claim of verse 35 look ridiculous. But it may be possible to understand this imminence differently. If, as was suggested in yesterday's notes, Jesus originally used 'son of man' language to refer to his own vindication, then it is the case that within a generation he was raised from the dead and Jerusalem was razed to the ground. Although Matthew reinterprets the coming of the Son of man, he retains the note of imminence out of faithfulness to the tradition of the sayings of Jesus. As we shall see in the following passages, Matthew expects the life of the world to continue for some time yet, before the Son of man eventually comes as the world's saviour and judge.

4   A call to alertness and wisdom   Read Matthew 24:45—25:13

What does Jesus mean when he calls his followers to 'watch' and 'be ready'? These two parables begin to spell out what Matthew understands by this. The first compares the Son of man to a householder (in marked contrast to the parable in v. 43, where he is a burglar!). The stewards are responsible for making sure that the rest of the household have what they need. They represent church leaders, who are to be 'faithful and wise' in their stewardship. If in the householder's absence they abuse their trust, they will end up like the tenants who mismanage the vineyard (21:33ff), sharing the fate of the hypocrites (cf chapter 23).

The second parable recalls a number of images already found in the Gospel—the marriage feast of 22:1–14, the bridegroom of 9:15–16, the lamps of 5:14–16, the cry of the foolish and the Lord's response in 7:21–23, and of course the delay motif of the previous parable. The scenario is a marriage celebration, where the bridegroom goes to collect the bride from her family home, before taking her to the house where they will live. There they meet the bride's attendants, and the others who share the celebrations with them. For some unknown reason, the couple are delayed (the alternative version of verse 1 includes the bride). Unlike their wise sisters, the foolish virgins have not brought enough oil to sustain them through the wait. The suggestion that they should see if the shops are open in the middle of the night (v. 9) has an air of absurdity about it, which only serves to heighten their folly.

Taken together, the two parables begin to unravel the meaning of watchful readiness. Wise church leaders will want to be like Peter, holding onto the confession of *Jesus* as 'the Christ, the Son of the Blessed', and resisting the attractions of alternatives. They will commend *his* teaching and example—the spirit of the Sermon on the Mount, the way of justice, mercy, faith and love—among his followers, and between the church and the wider world (including the synagogue). Wise church members will hold fast to the integrity of their words and deeds, weighing carefully what it means to live in absence of the bridegroom (see 9:15), and heeding Jesus' call to let the way they deal with distress and persecution dispel the darkness around them (see the notes on 5:10–16).

Being watchful and alert means paying attention to what is happening *outside*, in the wider world—without ignoring the impact of events on the *inside*, on the hearts and minds of believers, and in their common life. Whatever the circumstances in which the church lives out its faith, wise disciples will need to be awake to these connections between outer and inner life.

5 Determination or desperation? *Read Matthew 25:14–30*

The third parable uses the story of a wealthy entrepreneur to tease out further the meaning of alertness. It has the now-familiar motifs of a master's absence and delay, but it places more emphasis than the previous two on the responsibilities of those who wait for him to come. We should not allow popular interpretations of this parable to obscure the unpleasantness of its basic story-line. 'Talents' are easily read as 'gifts', which gives rise to the moral that is often drawn from the parable, that we should use to the full the gifts that God gives us. But what happens to our reading of the story if we begin with verse 24? Here the master is described as a 'hard man': his avarice has made him 'arrogantly inhumane' (Malina and Rohrbaugh). In his absence he expects his servants to increase his already vast wealth (a talent was a measure of silver equivalent to 15 years wages for a labourer—in today's terms at least £150,000). In the prevailing economic system this could only happen at the expense of others. When he returns he plays true to form, rewarding those servants who have imitated his greed and punishing the one who refused to play his rapacious game.

For all its seediness, the parable presses home a powerful message to the followers of Jesus. Just as its 'good and faithful' servants actively participated in their master's work while he was away, so the disciples of Jesus should show the same determination to be about *their* master's business while they wait for him to return. They must realize that Jesus has entrusted them with something of far greater value than silver. And if they are determined to 'trade' with his gospel, they will put its power to work in the world, thereby spreading its influence. Burying the talent is a sign of desperation, the result of losing hope in the power of the gospel to transform a world characterized by persecution and hatred, evil and violence. Like hiding a light under a bushel (5:15), irresponsible disciples only deprive the world of the illumination it desperately needs if it is to be redeemed.

Matthew uses this parable to invite his readers to ask searching questions about what it might mean to be 'good and faithful' servants. Do we have anything to learn about determined discipleship from today's agents of greed and self-interest?

6 Living wisely before God's surprising judgment
Read Matthew 25:31–46

The judgment scene at the climax of Jesus' final discourse picks up and develops earlier material from the parables in 13:41ff and 13:47ff, as well as amplifying 24:30–31. But the real interest here lies not so much in the *reality* of judgment as in its *rationale*. This is clear from the repetition in verses 35–45 of the deeds that lead to salvation or condemnation. We are told that prior to the Last Judgment the Son of man/King has appeared incognito before the nations of the world, in the guise of the victims of injustice, later referred to as 'the least of these my brethren'. Their identity has been extensively discussed by scholars. In view of the earlier designations of Jesus' disciples as 'brothers' (e.g. 12:49–50), it may be that the victims in mind here are persecuted disciples. But there are strong arguments in favour of a more general, universal application.

The judgment brings 'all the nations' before the Son of man's throne. The righteous are surprised when they are told that in helping the victims they have been ministering to the Son of man ('when did we see you...?' in vv. 37–39). It is more likely, then, that the parable identifies the Son of man with *all* victims of injustice. This means that everyone is destined to be judged by the way they respond to the needy. If we are surprised by the omission of any explicit Christian confession, we need only look back to Jesus' words in 5:6 and 7:21–23 (cf 22:40 and 23:23). On this understanding, Church members cannot take their salvation for granted: only the Day of Judgment will reveal the identity of the righteous.

What does it mean, then, to be ready for the coming of the Son of man? Faithful, wise and good servants of God's kingdom are determined to be about their Master's business, convinced that they will meet him when and where and in whom they least expect. In that encounter lies their salvation.

GUIDELINES

The end of Jesus' final discourse points backwards and forwards. It takes us back to the beginning of his first discourse—to the Beatitudes, and his promises to those who will have a place in the coming new world. If we read the beginning and the end together, we see what it means to live according to the spirit of the Beatitudes: nothing less than ministering to the needy, particularly the victims of oppression, persecution and violence.

The end also takes us forward to the Passion Narrative. We may wonder how it is that Jesus can be identified with the needy: when did *we* see him hungry, thirsty, a stranger, naked, sick, imprisoned? If we pay attention to the cross, we see one who is thirsty and naked, treated with the contempt and isolation reserved for the stranger. His body is sick with torment, its movement restricted in ways far worse than any imprisonment. There his solidarity with the oppressed is complete. To minister to the needy is, in some mysterious way, to serve the crucified Son of man.

17–23 MARCH   MATTHEW 26:1–75

1   Ugly intentions and a beautiful act   *Read Matthew 26:1–16*

At the start of Matthew's passion narrative, the action shifts between two scenes: the unofficial gatherings of members of the Jewish ruling council (in which the chief priests play a leading role), and the intimacy of the meal table, in the house where Jesus is presumably lodging during the Passover. Now that Jesus is in Jerusalem the chief priests replace the Pharisees as his opponents. They cannot afford to allow him free reign in the volatile atmosphere of the festival that celebrates Israel's liberation from foreign rule: their own position depends on keeping the peace. In case of any trouble, the Roman prefect always came to Jerusalem from Caesarea at Passover-tide with troop reinforcements. Jesus' teaching about the coming kingdom of God might suggest an alternative to the rule of Rome. Some of his Galilean sympathizers—no doubt in Jerusalem for the festival—are not averse to using violence to establish God's kingdom. Perhaps Jesus' action in the temple has only added to the stir created by his arrival in the city (21:10). The Jewish leaders cannot risk a further outbreak of unrest—hence their clandestine conversations.

The ugly violence they intend towards Jesus could not be more opposed to the beauty and tenderness of the woman's action in the house. It was customary for servants to wash the hands and feet of dinner guests, before anointing them with aromatic oils to remove bodily odours. Jesus sees her extravagance as devotion not waste. Without knowing it, she has performed a prophetic act. Perhaps Matthew intends us to see this as the human counterpart of Jesus' anointing with the Spirit at his baptism. If so, an anonymous woman (rather than the chief priest) has anointed Israel's messianic king, who will establish God's kingdom from the cross.

Judas was presumably one of the complaining disciples. His willingness to collude with the authorities takes us back to the other scene, where ugly violence is in the air. He is prepared to put Jesus into the hands of his enemies for a mere thirty pieces of silver, whereas the woman has 'wasted' a much greater sum on him. The contrasting actions of Judas and the woman point to the same end. And they also show where the real waste lies—not in a beautiful act of devotion, but in the series of cynical and ugly actions designed to remove an irritant from the system.

Throughout his passion narrative Matthew underlines the way that Jesus knows what will happen to him. He remains determined not to return violence for violence, even if that means letting his enemies take his life from him. Such is his devotion to the cause of God's kingdom, and the messianic power that will rule from the cross.

2   Solidarity in suffering and hope   *Read Matthew 26:17–29*

Passover started with the sacrifice of the lambs in the temple. That same evening, the seven-day Feast of Unleavened Bread began. Verses 17–19 suggest the need for secrecy in the face of danger: Jesus will travel into the city from Bethany later, under the cover of darkness. But the danger does not only lie outside the circle of his disciples. They are clearly shaken by Jesus' statement about betrayal by one of their number, and they wonder what he means. Matthew's additional words in verse 25 leave no doubt as to who and what Jesus has in mind.

At the supper, Jesus interprets the significance of what is about to happen to him. The evangelists omit most of the details of the Passover meal, to bring to the fore the new meaning that Jesus invests in the bread and wine. Like Moses killing the oxen and throwing their blood onto the people, Jesus' whole life-given-up-in-death is the sacrifice that seals the covenant between God and his people (see Exodus 24:1–8). Only Matthew has Jesus telling the disciples to 'eat' and 'drink', and referring to the forgiveness of sins (see Jeremiah 31:31–34; cf Matthew 1:21). Jesus' martyrdom will create a new covenant community which witnesses to God's forgiveness of sins by 'eating' and 'drinking' the body and blood of Jesus. 'Eating' and 'drinking' are powerful symbols of solidarity. Not only are Jesus' disciples to live by his teaching about mercy and non-violence, found throughout this gospel. They must also be ready for martyrdom (10:21; 16:24ff; 24:9), the ultimate identification with their Lord.

Since Jesus first began to speak about his passion in Galilee (17:22) he has used the image of the 'son of man' from Daniel 7. He does so once again in verse 24. He expects to suffer the fate of righteous Israel at the hands of the enemies of God's kingdom, but he will be vindicated as their representative. This suggests that Jesus sees his passion as the leading edge of the coming new world. He will not suffer in isolation, as he has repeatedly made clear. But those who identify with his cause can also expect to share in the blessings of the kingdom with him. This comes across in Jesus' final words at the meal, and to highlight this hope Matthew adds two very important words to Mark's version of verse 29: 'with you' (cf Mark 14:25). Eating and drinking *now* will have its counterpart in *the age to come*. Does this hope belong with your experience of holy communion?

3 Wide-awake prayer *Read Matthew 26:30–46*

In what follows, the disciples have their first opportunity to identify with Jesus in his suffering. He adapts words from Zechariah 13:7, to express his misgivings about their support. Their faith in him—the fragile trust that had been slowly and painfully built up over their time together—will finally crack under the severe testing it is about to face. Peter insists that he will stand firm. Jesus' contradiction only draws out a further promise of loyalty, now echoed by the other disciples.

Gethsemane (literally 'oil valley'), part of the Mount of Olives overlooking Jerusalem, gives the disciples a chance to prove the loyalty they profess. Presumably Jesus has noticed that Judas is missing, so he tells eight of the disciples to keep watch while he takes Peter, James and John with him to pray. Jesus knows he is in great danger, and naturally asks those closest to him to support him through it. The words he uses in verse 38 to express his feelings echo the repeating refrain in Psalms 42 and 43 (a single Psalm in the Hebrew Bible—see Psalm 42:5). In this time of crisis, can these disciples remember Jesus' earlier call to watch and be ready (24:42 and in the parables following)? Will they prove to be faithful, wise and good servants, while their master is but a short distance away praying?

Like the burgled householder (24:43) and the foolish virgins (25:5), Peter, James and John sleep. They appear to have lost sight of the importance of prayer in the face of temptation (6:13). But Jesus can only live as he prays, and pray as he lives. 'Father, the thought of being abandoned by my friends, rejected by my own people, and executed as a common criminal fills me with horror. If only this cup of sorrow and suffering could pass from me...'. Unlike the three disciples, Jesus is as awake to his own vulnerability as he is to the power of God. He finds enough strength to keep his weary flesh alert, as he continues to pray with integrity, 'Father... thy will be done'. Jesus' example of prayer in the face of trial and distress is just what his followers need if they are to find wisdom and strength so that they too can endure persecution (10:16ff; 24:9ff).

Wide-awake prayer, in which we recognize our vulnerability and submit to God's will and purpose, enables us to draw near to Jesus as he faces his darkest hour, and to draw on all that sustained him—nothing less than the strength and energy of God.

4 Scriptural patterns of responsibility *Read Matthew 26:47–56*

The violence and tenderness of this week's first reading return in this scene, though with heavy irony. Judas—who will make it possible for Jesus' enemies to carry out their ugly intentions—betrays Jesus with that universal symbol of tender affection, the kiss. And one of his companions (only in John 18:10 is he identified as Simon Peter), who must have heard Jesus' teaching about violence again and again, resorts to the sword. Jesus once again repudiates this kind of behaviour; even at his most vulnerable, he continues to warn about the danger of allowing violence to escalate.

Did Judas find it easy to answer the question that followed his affectionate greeting? Why *was* he there, at the head of an armed mob sent by Jesus' enemies? While Peter and the others had been taking their rest, he had been awake and alert. Peter's sleep was the precursor of his denial, but Judas' wakefulness gave him the opportunity for betrayal. Peter's sleep was a sign of his weakness; Judas' alertness symbolized his wilful rejection of the way of Jesus and the will of God. So why did Judas greet Jesus as his 'master'? In verses 54 and 56 Jesus refers once again to the fulfilment of scripture (see also vv. 24, 31). (It is ironic that those who until recently were struggling to stay awake now find the energy to flee!) Are Judas and the other disciples simply acting out parts that are already written for them? Indeed, we might ask the same question of Jesus.

There is nothing mechanical about the fulfilment of scripture in the story taking shape here. In this traditional Jewish way of speaking, Jesus understands himself and the people around him to be playing out the consequences of their respective attitudes to the will and purpose of God. Again and again the Hebrew scriptures recount the results of living faithfully before God—rejection, persecution and even death. Martyrdom is not so much a script written in advance, as the price Jesus has to pay for living as he prays: 'Father... your kingdom come, your will be done, on earth as it is in heaven.' Judas is as responsible for his behaviour as Jesus is for his. The difference is that one set of actions is based on outright rejection, the other on total acceptance of the way that brings God's salvation to the world.

Yesterday's reading showed Jesus as the exemplar of prayer; today's depicts him as the model of faithfulness to God. Underlying these are his commitment to prayer and his understanding of scripture—both are means of real communion with the living God.

111

At last Jesus and Caiaphas meet, for what is likely to have been an informal late-night hearing rather than a formal trial. According to John 11:47ff the decision to have Jesus executed was taken earlier, in his absence. The Sanhedrin probably did not have the legal authority to condemn anyone to death. The hearing would have enabled them to find a good reason for presenting Jesus to the Roman governor as worthy of execution.

The relevance of the testimony in verse 61 is not immediately apparent, because speaking against the temple was not a capital offence. (Note that in 23:38 and 24:2 Jesus did not say that *he* would bring down the temple, but implied that *God* would destroy it.) Likewise claiming to be the Messiah was no reason for execution. (Notice Jesus' reserve in verse 64; contrast Mark 14:62.) Some Jewish groups believed that the messiah would destroy or re-build the temple. If Jesus' prophetic action against the temple was understood as having messianic implications, this might explain the link between the testimony and the high priest's question, in which Matthew's readers will find echoes of Peter's confession in 16:16. (Note that Jesus' subsequent words to Peter in 16:18 about building his church on the rock of faith might imply a replacement for the Jerusalem temple and its rock.) Attitudes to the temple and aspirations to messiahship might well have gone hand in hand.

There is a deeper issue behind Caiaphas' question about the Messiah: who has the authority to speak and act for God, to set out the shape of Israel's salvation? Is Jesus claiming this? The most significant part of the exchange between Jesus and Caiaphas comes in the 'Son of man' saying verse 64. Why does the High Priest react like this? Matthew's version is slightly different from the other synoptics, in the reference to 'hereafter', which harks back to the judgment scene in 25:31–46. If Jesus is vindicated as 'Son of man', the tables will eventually be turned on his interrogators. On the last day they, not he, will find themselves on the receiving end of God's judgment, while his cause will triumph. From the high priest's perspective, it is blasphemy for this self-styled prophet from Galilee to claim such ultimate authority. If Jesus is right, God has no place for the purity system centred in the temple and its priesthood, or for a society organized around the priestly understanding of holiness as separation. Jesus' messianic vision is dangerously subversive, and the priestly élites stand to lose everything if it ever succeeds. It is hardly surprising that they see Jesus as a false prophet who deserves death (Deuteronomy 13:5)—and their cynical violence brings it that much nearer.

6 Remorse, repentance and suicide
Read Matthew 26:69—27:10

Peter has impressed us as a man of intense loyalty to Jesus. He cannot imagine his Lord as a victim of violence (16:22). Neither can he contemplate deserting Jesus in his hour of need (26:33). When Jesus is arrested the other disciples flee for their lives, but not Peter: he alone is brave enough to slip into the high priest's courtyard, where he can watch the events unfolding, hopefully unnoticed. But he does not remain unrecognized. Two maids identify him as one of Jesus' followers, and a group of people echo their conviction that Peter was 'with Jesus'. Having come so far, Peter now tries to distance himself further from Jesus, and his denials only increase in intensity. Once again we see Peter's tendency to buckle under pressure when his own safety is at risk (cf 14:30)—something Jesus must have known only too well.

Peter's threefold denial is an object lesson for Christians enduring opposition. His feelings for Jesus clearly run deep: his tears of remorse are evidence enough. But deep feelings are no substitute for the deeply rooted faith (13:21) that is fed by prayer. Three times in Gethsemane Peter had missed the opportunity to pray with Jesus, and so find the strength he needed to overcome temptation. Prayer is necessary if the Holy Spirit is to do his work (10:19–20), and if the community under pressure is to support itself (24:9–10).

Like Peter, Judas too regrets his actions as he sees events unfolding. His repentant tone in verses 3–4 suggests that he is surprised by the outcome of his betrayal. Does he think he can save Jesus by protesting his innocence? Or is he merely trying to salve his own conscience? Matthew's account of Judas is more sympathetic than Luke's (see Acts 1:18ff). Perhaps Judas had tried to engineer a meeting between Jesus and the chief priests, without thinking that his thirty pieces of silver were the price of innocent blood. Matthew is as ingenious as ever in finding scriptural echoes in the outcome of Judas' tragedy, though the links with Jeremiah are strained (see Zechariah 11:12–13, which may have been part of the material associated with Jeremiah at this time).

Peter's remorse, Judas' repentance and suicide—together they indicate the depth of feeling for Jesus in these two men. They also show how essential it is to feed such feeling by prayerful faith, rooted in what Jesus has been saying throughout the Gospel about his way of being God's Messiah. Feeling divorced from the way of Christ can lead to failure, and even tragedy.

GUIDELINES

This week's readings present us with a wide range of responses to Jesus: tenderness and violence, promises of loyalty and denial, betrayal and outright condemnation. What they have in common is the depth of feeling they reveal towards Jesus, either for or against him.

A familiar narrative like this can act as a mirror for our own responses to Jesus. While we may be more like Peter than the high priest, we do well to consider the depth of feeling we have for Jesus and his cause. How much do Jesus, and all that he stands for, really matter to you?

24–30 MARCH   MATTHEW 27:11—28:20

1 When self-interest wins the day   *Read Matthew 27:11–26*

Pilate's opening question is found in all four Gospels, which suggests that Jesus is presented to him as a messianic pretender (something only Luke 23:2 makes explicit). He answers Pilate as he had earlier replied to the high priest's question (26:64). 'You have said so' might mean 'the words are yours'—Jesus neither admits nor denies anything. He is just as silent before his accusers here as he was earlier (26:63). Pilate accepts this as an invitation to have a little sport with the chief priests and the crowds outside. He believes that the real reason why the Jewish leaders have brought Jesus to him is his popularity. Perhaps he can persuade the crowds, then, to call for Jesus' release and snub the authority of their leaders. But he reckons without the determination and cunning of Jesus' accusers.

Why could the chief priests persuade people to call for Barabbas rather than Jesus? If the crowds were drawn from among the inhabitants of Jerusalem, they would have a lot to lose if this Galilean who spoke and acted against the temple were given the freedom of the city. Most of Jerusalem's economy was based on the temple, which employed thousands of priests and craftsmen in what one writer has called a great job-creation scheme! The crowd's call for Barabbas is an understandable expression of their self-interest, which the chief priests manage to exploit for their own ends. Whether or not Pilate is convinced that Jesus really is a messianic pretender, he has no doubts about his power to disturb the peace of Jerusalem.

The sport has to stop: Pilate's game-plan risks a riot that he can hardly afford. Questions would be asked higher up the chain of command. So the governor too must allow his self-interest to win the day—but not without washing his hands of the affair (only in Matthew). Though Matthew is keen to depict the chief priests as the prime movers in Jesus' execution (aided and abetted by the mob), Pilate is not entirely without blame. He comes across as one who shows little real interest in the people at the centre of Jerusalem's affairs. If Jesus' execution preserves the peace and gets him off the hook, then so be it.

Notice two other features unique to Matthew's account. The intervention of Pilate's wife serves to underline Jesus' innocence (cf 27:4)—perhaps we are meant to interpret her dream as a message from God! The crowd's response to Pilate's public hand-washing in verse 25 is variously interpreted. Some see it as another anti-Jewish streak in Matthew: because the Jewish people as a whole ('all the people') are responsible for Jesus' execution, God will take vengeance on them (presumably by destroying the temple: see 23:35–39). Alternatively it might be an ironic remark: though the crowds certainly play their part in sending Jesus to the cross, the Jewish people are among those who will benefit from his death. God's new covenant, sealed with Jesus' blood (26:28), will establish itself among the Jewish people, as well as embracing the Gentiles.

2 Mockery, irony and truth   *Read Matthew 27:27–44*

Once Pilate has washed his hands of Jesus, his soldiers can take over. Jesus is treated just like any other prisoner in detention. Weakened now after the scourging and torture that preceded execution, he is an easy target for the guards' contempt and brutality. They gather the 600-strong battalion to witness the humiliation that started in the high priest's house (26:67f), and continued before Pilate and the crowds. What began in Galilee as an attempt to undermine Jesus' credibility (see 12:24) is completed here in Jerusalem, in the public degradation of the cross.

Jesus has been passed to the soldiers as a would-be king, so they play a dressing-up game with him. They give him symbols of his presumed authority—one of their cloaks, and an improvised crown and sceptre—and then attack him cynically with the reed. The restraint in the narrative obscures the extent of the brutality Jesus has to endure. But he is clearly too weak now to carry his own cross. The offer of 'wine mixed with gall' to dull the pain is a small gesture of kindness before Jesus is stripped naked and executed. The charge on the inscription is intended to deter other would-be Jewish messiahs. Crucifixion was an important way of subjugating an occupied people, and it reminded the Jews of their subservience to the authority of Rome. If the public humiliation of Jesus is now complete, the execution of another Jew can hardly bring unalloyed delight to Israel as a whole.

Some Jews, however, do revel in the shaming of Jesus. The passers-by in verses 39–40 may be inhabitants of Jerusalem who rejoice at the demise of one who threatened their way of life. The Jewish leaders have at last achieved their ambition. Why those crucified beside Jesus should revile him is anyone's guess (only Luke refers to the penitent thief). Matthew makes some significant additions to verse 40 in the phrase 'if you are the Son of God', and verse 43 is only found here. We are reminded of Jesus' temptations in the wilderness, where he proved his faithfulness as God's Son. The journey to the cross has sorely tested Jesus' loyalty to God. His execution might look like humiliation and disgrace, but Matthew presents it as the epitome of trust in God. This is highlighted further by scriptural allusions (e.g. Psalm 22:18; Psalm 69:21; Wisdom 2:12–20) which allow the evangelist to present Jesus as the truly faithful Israelite.

There is irony as well as insult in Jesus' mockery and humiliation. He *is* the messiah—'the king of the Jews' and 'the Son of God'; and he *cannot save himself* by coming down from the cross. The true power of *this* Messiah (and of the God he represents) lies in his willingness to *give himself* utterly for God's cause. As we heard just before Jesus entered Jerusalem, true liberation lies in the way of the servant (20:28).

3 What is God doing in the crucifixion of Jesus?
Read Matthew 27:45–56

Matthew spares us the details of Jesus' suffering: it is enough to underline the reality of Jesus' death. The cry of dereliction and the scream of pain as he dies (both only here and in Mark) bring us as close as we can get to his anguish. Like anyone else in what was until now unimaginable pain, Jesus wonders where God is. He utters the only words he knows to express his sense of total abandonment: 'my God, my God, why have you forsaken me' (Psalm 22:1).

Matthew uses scripture to highlight his paradoxical conviction that the *presence* of God is brought into the sharpest possible focus in this place of abandonment. The darkness at noon draws on Amos 8:9–10: the sun sets at midday on the day when God comes to judge his people, making the feast day like 'the mourning for an only son'. Illuminating the dying figure are the Psalms of the righteous sufferer (22, 69), with their confidence in God's persistent commitment to his faithful ones, despite the opposition they face from their enemies. Only Matthew alludes to resurrection scriptures (Isaiah 26:19; Ezekiel 37:11–12; Daniel 12:1ff) in verses 52–53, to depict the outcome of Jesus' passion. This biblical tapestry displays the evangelist's understanding of what God is doing in the crucifixion of Jesus.

The parable of the rebellious tenants in 21:33ff is also worth re-reading at this point (see notes, page 95). As Jesus dies, the darkness of divine judgment descends on those who have cast the son out of the vineyard and killed him. The age of the temple is now over—its curtain is torn from top to bottom, leaving the Holy Place wide open to 'other tenants'. Soon to appear is the age of resurrection, the kingdom of God, in which Israel becomes a new covenant people of Jew and Gentile (symbolized by Galilean women and the Roman centurion). The divine power that governs the age of salvation is embodied in this 'king of the Jews': the redeeming power of self-sacrifice, the standard by which the whole world is to be judged (25:31–46).

Little if anything of this would have been evident at the time: the women who saw it all from a distance would have been distraught at the brutality visited on their beloved Jesus. The hindsight that comes from faith is responsible for weaving the tapestry that Matthew holds up for us to contemplate.

We adore you, O Christ, and we bless you. For by your holy cross you have redeemed the world.

4   Preparing for Easter with confidence and security
Read Matthew 27:57–66

Matthew concludes his passion narrative with these two scenes, connected by their association with the dead body of Jesus. Joseph of Arimathea is mentioned in all four Gospels, though his details differ. In Mark and Luke, he is a member of the Jewish ruling council who was looking for the kingdom of God (was he then a Pharisee?). Luke tells us that he did not concur with Jesus' death. In John and Matthew, Joseph is a disciple of Jesus (though secretly in John). Only in Matthew is he described as a 'rich man'. In all four Gospels, he arranges for Jesus' burial (with the help of Nicodemus in John), though only Matthew mentions that the tomb is his, perhaps alluding to Isaiah 53:9. (Tombs like this have been excavated outside Jerusalem.) Matthew, Mark and Luke refer to the women at the tomb: because they see where Jesus' body is laid, they will be able to identify the place with confidence.

Only Matthew refers to Joseph placing a '*great* stone' over the entrance to the tomb. This, together with the reference to the guard on the tomb (again only in Matthew), suggests that the evangelist is intent on countering a rival explanation for the empty tomb on 'the third day'. Alongside 28:15, verse 64 suggests that rumours were rife (in the synagogues known to Matthew?) that the disciples had stolen Jesus' body and circulated the story that God had raised him from the dead. But it is hardly likely that the very disciples who had struggled throughout their time with Jesus to share his confidence in the power of God, and had deserted and denied him before his execution, could have perpetrated such a fraud so soon after Jesus' death, if at all. This makes the account in verses 62–66 historically improbable, though its apologetic purpose is clear enough. Perhaps Matthew is using the great stone and the guards to say that whatever else happened to the body of Jesus once it had been placed in the tomb, it could not have been stolen by his followers.

For Matthew, the very security of the tomb and the confidence with which it could be identified allow only one explanation for the disappearance of Jesus' body, as we shall see in tomorrow's reading.

5 The uncomplicated joy of Easter *Read Matthew 28:1–10*

All the Gospel accounts of Easter morning tell us that Mary Magdalene went to Jesus' tomb early on the Sabbath day (in John she goes alone). The witness of these Galilean women is clearly important in the Gospel tradition—they are the first messengers of the resurrection—though Paul does not mention them in 1 Corinthians 15:5ff. Matthew's narrative is based on Mark's, though there are some significant differences of detail. In addition to the guards, only Matthew has an earthquake (cf 27:51); Mark's young man becomes a glorious angel from heaven (cf 1:20; 2:13, 19), who rolls back the stone. Matthew also has the risen Jesus appearing to the women, though his words only reiterate what the angel has told them.

The most striking difference between Matthew and Mark is one of mood. For one thing Matthew slackens the tension in the story. The women do not wonder how they are going to get into the tomb to anoint Jesus' body, as they do in Mark. They simply come to see the sepulchre, almost as if they know what they will find there. Furthermore, where Mark is mysterious and enigmatic, Matthew is clear and straightforward. We saw earlier how, in his intimation of the outcome of Jesus' passion, Matthew began to turn up the temperature of anticipation and hope (see especially 27:52ff). We might wonder whether this approach allows something of the mystery of Easter to evaporate. As a result, Matthew is more 'matter-of-fact' than Mark. The guards might be overwhelmed by the angelic appearance, but the women take it all in their stride. They hardly seem surprised at all by what the angel tells them. Where Mark's women are utterly dumbfounded, Matthew's can hardly contain their joy.

For Matthew the empty tomb can only signify one thing: an unambiguously divine event is responsible for what has happened. There is no room for shock or grief, no space for faith to grow and develop. Doubtless Matthew has his reasons for presenting the Easter story as he does. But alongside his exuberance, it is good to have Mark's mystery, Luke's gradual discovery and John's acknowledgment of the pain of losing someone close. Without the other evangelists, Matthew's Easter story might seem brash and forced. Read together, though, the four evangelists provide us with a more rounded picture of the Easter faith, to which Matthew's uncomplicated joy makes a necessary contribution.

6   Easter faith and integrity   *Read Matthew 28:11–20*

While the women look for Jesus' male disciples, the guards recover from their angel-induced shock and report all that has happened to the Jewish authorities. Their readiness to suppress the truth by resorting to bribery only presents them in a bad light: their integrity leaves much to be desired. Once again (cf 27:62ff) we are in the realms of counter-propaganda, more attuned to the circumstances of Matthew's day than the events of the first Easter.

Matthew's conclusion has a number of important elements. Jesus' appearance in Galilee makes this the region where *promise is fulfilled*. Scattered disciples are gathered together (see 26:32), and Gentiles can hope to be included in Israel's salvation (see 4:12ff). So Galilee makes an ideal location for the 'great commission' in verse 19. The reference to doubt in verse 17 reminds us of Thomas in John 20:24ff, but the overwhelming mood here is one of *worship* (cf 2:11; 28:9 and John 20:28—again Thomas). This is an entirely appropriate response to the *authority of Jesus*, which God has now endorsed by raising him from the dead. What Jesus had claimed throughout his ministry in relation to Israel—the right to speak and act for God—is now universalized by the resurrection. Jesus is given nothing less than the authority of Daniel's 'son of man' (see Daniel 7:14), which suggests that the life of the world will reflect the intention of its creator whenever it is guided and shaped by all that we have seen and heard in Jesus. This is why he *commissions* his followers to extend their own calling to 'all nations' (contrast 10:5–6; 15:24). Worship and worldwide mission are therefore integral to the Easter faith.

Verse 20 takes us back to 1:23, to underline the integrity of Christmas and Easter: God is with us in the whole story of Jesus. By the end of the Gospel we can see that 'us' means *all*: Gentile as well as Jew, woman as well as man, child as well as adult, despised as well as honoured, sinner as well as righteous. The life of discipleship cannot proceed without looking for, and serving, the Easter presence of God, however surprisingly and unexpectedly it may come upon us (25:37ff). This is the only way of living responsibly as we wait for the appearance of the Master.

GUIDELINES

Easter is traditionally a time for baptism. Matthew's Gospel ends with the command to baptize disciples 'in the name of the Father and of the Son and of the Holy Spirit'. In the light of the story we have just finished, what does this suggest?

• *In the name of the Father: the Father of Jesus is the creator of the world, whose essential character is indiscriminate mercy, and whose care invites our trust and dependence.*

• *... and of the Son: Jesus the Son reveals the response God looks for from all people—readiness to live by faith, to eschew violence, and to face suffering for the sake of God's kingdom with courage and hope.*

• *...and of the Holy Spirit: the Spirit of God anointed Jesus at his baptism, enabled him to live faithfully before God his Father, and inspires the Church in its witness.*

Baptism 'in the name of the Father and of the Son and of the Holy Spirit' draws us into the way of Jesus narrated in the Gospel of Matthew. What might this mean for you and your church this Easter?

Further reading

Margaret Davies, *Matthew*, JSOT, Sheffield Academic Press, 1993

Leslie Houlden, *Backward into Light. The Passion and Resurrection of Jesus according to Matthew and Mark*, SCM Press, 1987

Jack Dean Kingsbury, *Matthew As Story*, second edition, Fortress Press, 1988

Bruce J. Malina and Richard L. Rohrbaugh, *Social Science Commentary on the Synoptic Gospels*, Fortress Press, 1992

Graham Stanton, *A Gospel For A New People. Studies in Matthew*, T. & T. Clark, 1992

The Revelation to John

If any book needs a health warning it is Revelation, with its horrific pictures of demonic destruction and divine vengeance. But it is the true climax of the whole Bible and we must not leave it to cranks and those who read it as predicting contemporary events in the Middle East.

Read Revelation 1:1–3

It is, first, a revelation, *apocalypse*, which means 'uncovering'—unmasking, taking the lid off. 'Apocalyptic' has links with satire and political cartoons. It can comfort the afflicted, but also afflict the comfortable. Secondly it is prophecy—not just prediction but God's word breaking urgently into the present as through Amos or Isaiah, sharp to the complacent. 'Blessed are those who hear': many would not have wanted to.

Thirdly it is a letter, 'John to the seven churches in the province of Asia' (1:4), and to understand a letter you need to know the circumstances. John was writing probably at the end of the first century AD. Older folk would have vivid memories of Nero's massacre of Christians in 64, the civil wars of 68–69 when the empire seemed on the verge of collapse, and the Roman destruction of Jerusalem in 70. But many would not remember. In Asia Rome was popular. The cities had enthusiastic cults of the goddess Rome and the divine emperor. Not to join in would be suspicious, if not treasonable. The messages to the churches in chapters 2 and 3 paint a mixed picture of heroic fidelity and creeping compromise, but it is the latter which predominates. The violence of John's pictures is to shock Christians awake who are dazzled by Roman civilization and achievements—compare the so-called 'German Christians' dazzled by Hitler in the thirties, and Bonhoeffer's appeal to Revelation.

John's visions spring from deep meditation on scripture, echoing its language, and from deep meditation on Christ crucified. He in effect turns all the vindictiveness and violence upside down by showing the Lion of Judah as a sacrificial Lamb (5:6). Revelation, for all its bewildering changes of scene, is a closely knit whole. Large sections taken on their own are ghastly, but we need to see them as part of the whole: enclosing the destructions of chapters 6–20 are the pictures of God, Creator and Redeemer, in 4–5 and 21:1—22:5. The corruption of earth, 'Babylon', is annihilated in grisly detail, so as to be redeemed in the new Jerusalem.

Any commentary on poetry is in danger of spoiling it; we should read (aloud) and listen to the book as a whole, as they would first have done. But they would have gone on to explore its intricate detail of scriptural reference. We who are less familiar with scripture may value guidance, but please feel free to pass over the cross-references in the notes that follow.

These notes are based on the Revised Standard Version (RSV), with reference also to the Revised English Bible (REB). It will not be possible to comment on every verse, or do justice to opposing views. This will be a one-sidedly *Christian* reading.

---

31 MARCH–6 APRIL   REVELATION 1:1—5:14

1   On the Lord's Day: John's Letter to the Church
Read Revelation 1:4–18

It begins like one of Paul's letters, 'Paul to the church at... , grace to you and peace from... ', but in deliberately barbarous Greek, as if 'from the Is and the Was and the Coming One'. God is, eternally and dynamically, always breaking into an unaware world. The 'seven spirits' echo Zechariah 4:2 and 10, suggesting God's manifold presence rather than his holy separateness. 'Faithful witness' and 'first-born' echo the messianic Psalm 89:26–27, 37, read in the light of Jesus' resurrection. His liberating love lies behind all the severity that follows towards his royal priesthood, the vocation God gave to Israel at Sinai (Exodus 19:6). Verse 7 brings together Daniel 7:13 and Jesus before Caiaphas (Mark 14:62) with Zechariah 12:10, 'they will look on him whom they have pierced and lament over him'—penitent recognition, not mere remorse (in REB). This positive hint points beyond all the negativity that follows.

Who was John? Son of Zebedee and author of the Fourth Gospel, Christians soon assumed, but all he tells us is that he was a 'prophet' (22:9), and was on Patmos, perhaps in preventive detention because of his preaching. There was no danger in being a Christian if you lay low. The 'Lord's Day' is both the final Day of the Lord and its anticipation in Jesus' rising from the dead on the first day of the week, Sunday, when Christians celebrated the eucharist; in worship heaven and earth, past, present and future, are one.

Seven is the number of completeness; these congregations represent the whole Church. The cities were all centres of communication, on a circular route—and centres of the emperor cult. John's opening vision of the human figure of Daniel 7 (representing God's faithful few), who dethrones the beasts (representing world empires), is in conscious contrast with imperial pretensions. The details come from many sources; a Bible with marginal references, or a commentary, enables one to follow up the allusions. They build a dynamic rather than photographic impression, appealing to ear not eye: we are not to visualize the sword coming out of his mouth (the piercing truth of God's word, Hebrews 4:12), any more than a hand on John's head holding seven stars (Christ's control of the planetary powers, or angels, which ruled human destiny—astrology then was deadly serious). Hades was both the king and the realm of the dead. By dying Jesus had won control even of death (Hebrews 2:14–15)— this is the true 'ruler of kings on earth'.

2 The Lord of the Churches *Read Revelation 1:19–2:11*

'What must take place hereafter' echoes Daniel 2:45, and like Daniel and Zechariah, John has things explained to him. The seven-branched candelabrum, the *menorah*, in the Jerusalem temple was a symbol of Israel, God's witnesses (Isaiah 43:10–12), his light for the nations. John sees seven separate lamps, together representing God's Israel, the Church, whose light is meant to shine before others (Matthew 5:16). But who are 'the angels of the churches'? Stars were thought to be angelic powers; each nation had its spiritual counterpart or 'prince' (Daniel 10:20, 21); individuals had their angels (Matthew 18:10; Acts 12:15). So the angel is the church as a spiritual whole, rather than a collection of different people.

Christ introduces each message with a motif from the opening vision, working backwards; thus he speaks to Ephesus as Lord of the churches, not an absentee but in among them and knowing them inside out. Ephesus vied with Pergamum as chief city of Asia and chief centre of the emperor cult. Paul had worked there (Acts 18 and 19). It had a strong tradition of Christian activity and a sharp nose for false teaching—we will hear more of the Nicolaitans at Pergamum—but it had let go its early love. Sound but censorious (cf 1 Corinthians 13)? Or lack of witness, as verse 5 and the lamp metaphor suggest? It has fallen (angels and stars were identified) and must repent. Were they self-righteously surprised? 'He who has an ear' is a reminder of Jesus' disturbing parables (Mark 4:9 etc.). 'To him who conquers': this is a key word, a metaphor from war, athletics and the law court, but turned upside down by Jesus' death (Revelation 5:5–6). The 'tree of life' was a symbol both of the tree of the cross and the fruit of that tree in the eucharist—something the Ephesians already enjoyed and perhaps took to be a guarantee of salvation. But they have fallen—outside the garden.

Smyrna, on the other hand, up the coast on the circular route a messenger would follow, is truly inside, for all its outward poverty. Jews had good reason to resent Christians who often stole their sympathizers ('godfearers') by offering what looked like cut-price salvation; 'slander' suggests legal accusation. But 'synagogue of Satan' is not 'anti-Semitic'. It refers to what they are *doing*. Satan is 'the accuser of the brethren' (12:10), God's opponent; Jesus could call Peter Satan (Matthew 16:23). It is even possible that these were Judaizing *Christians*, claiming to be the true synagogue and persecuting Christians who did not keep the Jewish Law. Language like this, taken out of context, has done enormous harm.

Smyrna's faithfulness unto death will win life (cf Mark 8:35). The 'second death' was a Jewish term for the final fate, after judgment, of those opposed to God.

3   Idolatry and fornication   *Read Revelation 2:11–29*

Pergamum was the capital of the pre-Roman kingdom, centre of the cult of Asclepius, god of healing, whose symbol was a serpent, and of the emperor cult—throne of Satan, the ancient serpent (12:9) in another guise. To abstain from the local cults would be suspicious; to testify against them might be suicidal. They had a good record of loyalty (notice that Antipas is the only acutal martyr mentioned in the messages, and that in the past), but now there is a move to conform. Balaam had put Balak up to tempting the Israelites as they came out of desert austerity into the Promised Land (Numbers 31:16 and 25:1–9); fornication is a regular metaphor for religious infidelity, and eating meat, which might have come from a pagan sacrifice, was to many Christians equivalent to idolatry. We know nothing directly about the Nicolaitans, but can guess they appealed to Paul's nuanced acceptance of 'meat sacrificed to idols' (1 Corinthians 8–10), and commendation of the 'powers that be' in Romans 13. Like the 'German Christians' in the thirties and South African supporters of apartheid they were no doubt sincere, even if (in John's view) diabolically wrong. For the two-edged sword see 1:16, over against the Roman governor's 'power of the sword'. The hidden manna is a symbol of the eucharist, the real 'meat' which Christ gives.

Thyatira was a mercantile city. It had many trade-guilds, with their religious rituals. To opt out could be economic suicide. The church is doing exceptionally well, in marked contrast to theologically sound Ephesus (2:19, cf 2:4–5)—except for 'Jezebel' (1 Kings 16:31–19:3; 2 Kings 9:22). Like Balaam, this is an offensive way of characterizing a powerful and no doubt sincere religious leader. The threats to her and her children are not to our taste, but compare the severity of Paul's language in 1 Corinthians 11:29–30. Issues of truth, and compromise, can be deadly serious, as in Hitler's Germany. Do we take them seriously enough? Or is there a danger in seeing things too black and white?

4 Lukewarm *Read Revelation 3*

Sardis, the capital of Croesus, was impregnable, but twice had been captured through complacency and sleep—remember Jesus' parable of the burglar (Matthew 24:43), and the returning master (Luke 12:35–40). At Sardis the church looked good, but was mostly rotten, though a few were 'worthy' (a key word in chapters 4 and 5). 'I will confess his name', in the light of Luke 12:8, suggests the rest were not confessing.

There are impressive remains of the great synagogue at Sardis, but no mention of Jewish opposition—unlike at Philadelphia. It shares the same pressures, and praise, as Smyrna. The promise in verse 12 is against the background of frequent evacuation because of earthquakes (common then as now in Turkey). It anticipates the final visions—the New Jerusalem which *comes* down, not just to come. It is already a present reality for faith, but one which can be lost, like paradise at Ephesus. 'Hold fast your crown', perhaps a symbol of baptismal belonging. It is possible to write yourself out of the book of life (3:5), but there is always the call to repent.

The climactic message takes up the theme of witness from 1:5.

Laodicea was a proudly prosperous city, and the church was doing brilliantly in a worldly way, but in contrast with impoverished Smyrna its riches were bogus. The lukewarm water, from the hot springs of Pammukale, suggests not the spiritual temper of the Laodiceans but the barrenness of their 'works'—their lack of witness. The promise at verse 20 evoked Holman Hunt's picture in Keble College chapel of Christ knocking at a handleless door. Think rather of the returning bridegroom who makes the servants who *open* at his *knock* sit down at table (Luke 12:35–37), and the bridegroom in the Song of Songs (5:1–2) knocking at the door of the sleeping bride. Five out of seven churches receive severe warnings for their lack of witness—from the faithful witness who loves us and has died to free us from our sins (1:5–6).

5 Rainbow and Sea *Read Revelation 4*

'Heaven open' is the hallmark of apocalyptic, the veil between heaven and earth drawn back (see Ezekiel 1:1; Mark 1:10; John 1:51; Acts 7:56). 'What must take place after this' takes us back to the beginning, creation; in heaven past, present and future are one. In the Bible the future is rooted in the past, and stories about the End and about the Beginning are to illuminate the Now. John never describes God. The throne on which he is seated is the source of authority and power, shared now with Jesus (3:21), in contrast with Satan's throne (2:13), which to John's hearers loomed so large. The jewels are there for sound as much as sight—they will be heard again in chapter 21. They are not merely decorative, least of all the *rainbow*, a crucial sign that in all the destructions to follow God has not forgotten his promise to Noah (Genesis 9:11–16). It figures in Ezekiel's vision of the chariot-throne (1:28), which was linked with Genesis and lies behind this whole chapter. The twenty-four elders perhaps represent the twelve apostles of the new covenant and the twelve patriarchs of the old. There are hints of the Sinai covenant in the *son et lumière* of verse 5 (Exodus 19:16), and of the Red Sea (v. 6; cf 15:2–3).

But this *sea* is many other things. Glass was rare, and beautiful. Crystal ('ice' in Greek) echoes the 'terrible crystal' (Ezekiel 1:22) of the firmament. The Flood came from the waters above the firmament and below the earth: the sea is the source of life but also of chaos and evil. It is a dragon (Rahab). Out of it come Daniel's four beasts and the beast of Revelation 13. In the new heaven and new earth there is no more sea (Revelation 21:1). But here it is in the present heaven, like the dragon Satan himself (12:7), a symbol of the freedom God allows for his creation to be corrupted—an ambivalence which he will finally overcome (Revelation 12:11).

The four living creatures from Ezekiel 1 offer the praises of creation with the 'trishagion' of Isaiah 6, which figured early in the eucharistic liturgy.

6 Lion and Lamb *Read Revelation 5*

Like the sea, the scroll is many interlocking things: the sealed book of Daniel 12:4; the tablets of destiny; the Torah scroll in the synagogue; a legal document with seals, such as might have on the outside a summary of the contents within, which the breaking of the seals makes operative; and thus Ezekiel's scroll (2:10), written on front and back with words of disaster (Revelation 6:1ff.). Biblical imagery is kaleidoscopic, evocative, open-ended, inviting the reader's own perceptions.

'No one worthy' echoes 4:11; only God can reveal the things of God. The good news is that one has been found—note again the keyword 'conquered'. 'Lion of Judah' (Genesis 49:9–11) and 'root of David' (Isaiah 11:1–10) are traditional images of the militant Messiah the Jews were expecting. That is what John hears. But what he sees is a sacrificial Lamb. Again there are interlocking meanings: the militant young ram of Jewish apocalyptic; the defenceless lamb of Jeremiah 11:19 and Isaiah 53:7–9; the lamb of sin-offering; above all the Passover Lamb, whose death ransomed Israel from Egypt to be a kingdom and priests (Revelation 5:9, 10). Jesus was 'the Lamb of God that takes away the sin of the world' and died when the Passover lambs were being slain (John 1:29; 19:31). This transposition of slaying lion into sacrificed lamb must make us transpose all the violence that follows.

The lamb is standing, like the Son of man Stephen saw (Acts 7:56). He went, like the Son of man to the Ancient of Days (Daniel 7:13), to take the scroll. His seven horns and eyes represent not only the fulness of power and wisdom, but also the paradoxical power and wisdom of God (1 Corinthians 1:24). The seven spirits (1:4) are now his eyes. 'Spirit' is neuter but 'sent out' (*apestalmenoi*) is masculine— people (apostles). Jesus is inseparable from his faithful witnesses— and from his Father: 'Worthy art thou... worthy is the lamb' (cf 4:11).

Jesus shares both the throne (3:21) and the praises of God himself.

GUIDELINES

'The chief end of humankind is to glorify God and enjoy him for ever'. Idolatry, the worship of what is not God (however sincerely we may believe it to be God), is the root of the world's evils. In worship men and women are most truly themselves; the 'veil of sense' that 'hangs dark between' us and God is most nearly pierced as we join with angels and archangels and all the company of heaven. Not that we can see God. 'John knows that to ordinary mortals the presence of God becomes real not through direct vision, even in the mind's eye, but through the impact of those to whom God is the supreme reality. So he allows his readers to look on the Eternal Light through the mirror of the worshipping host of heaven' (G.B. Caird, *The Revelation of St John the Divine*, page 63).

7–13 APRIL   REVELATION 6:1—14:20

1   **Unsealing the scroll: sealing God's Israel**
    Read Revelation 6 and 7

The lamb's victorious death should make things better, but opening the scroll makes them worse—'lamentation, mourning and woe' (Ezekiel 2:10)—as for Israel after the Exodus (Numbers 14:2). The cry 'Come!' (*Marana tha*) must, in a rebellious world, bring disaster. The four horsemen in Zechariah (1:8–15, 6:1–8) were God's agents for punishing the nations. They bring natural disasters, in terms drawn from the prophets (Jeremiah 14:12; Ezekiel 14:21, etc.) and based on Jesus' apocalypse (Mark 13; Matthew 24; Luke 21)—except for the first. 'White' is the colour of heaven; 'crowns' and 'conquering' suggest the martyrs and the triumphant progress of the gospel. But can the gospel be aligned with war, famine and pestilence? Most commentators think it must be conquest in the bad sense (the bow was the weapon of the dreaded Parthians), as a Satanic parody of Christ's final coming: see 19:11–16. But the gospel *is* disaster for those wrapped up in their own concerns; see 11:4–10; 14:6–7.

The fifth seal presents the cry of all the seemingly wasted suffering from Abel on; God has a plan and it must take its course (cf Colossians 1:24). The sixth seal takes us in anticipation to the End, with imagery of the Day of the Lord from scripture and from the road to Calvary where the Day began (Hosea 10:8; Luke 23:28–31). Christians live between 'D Day' and 'V Day'. But 'the wrath of the Lamb': where is love and forgiveness here? Love to the estranged can be torment (11:10). If God is God, and if all screens are removed, his presence must be grace or wrath, no middle ground. The words of verse 16 come from the impenitent, out of their delusion. In Francis Thompson's words: 'Tis ye, tis your estrangèd faces, that miss the many-splendoured thing.'

The opening of the scroll unleashes the first of three series of seven disasters on earth, each followed by a heavenly interlude. After the unsealing comes the sealing of God's servants. Then as now a seal meant ownership and protection; it was a metaphor for baptism (cf 2 Corinthians 1:22). Not protection from physical harm, as chapter 6 showed, but from spiritual attack. The 'four winds' suggest demonic powers (Daniel 7:2ff.) and the 'great tribulation' (Revelation 3:10), out of which the 'great multitude' will have come (7:14).

But what is their relation to the 12,000 from each tribe, the 144,000? Jewish Christians and Gentile Christians? But for John, as for Paul, all Christians, Jew and Gentile, now make up the Israel of God. The clue again lies in hearing and seeing. John hears the theological truth 'salvation is from the Jews' (John 4:22); he sees a countless throng, in fulfilment of the promise to Abraham (Genesis 15:5; 22:17). The two groups are the same, from different points of view.

The psalms point to the Jewish harvest feast of Tabernacles. It symbolized God's final dwelling with his people, as once he dwelt with them in tents on their dangerous journey through the desert. The imagery comes from Isaiah's picture of the new exodus from Babylon and journey back to Zion (49:10; cf 25:8).

2 The seven trumpets, summons to repentance
Read Revelation 8 and 9

The opening of the seventh seal introduces a new series of disasters. The enigmatic silence in heaven may be, according to a Jewish tradition, for the prayers of earth to be heard (8:4), or it may be the primeval silence out of which issues the word of God for creation, and new creation (2 Esdras 7:29ff.). Trumpet is another word with multiple associations: liturgy, war, warning, the Day of the Lord. On New Year's Day trumpets initiated a penitential season leading up to the Day of Atonement.

These visions still do not give the contents of the scroll. They are warning blasts, dramatic pictures of the world's idolatry destroying the world, vainly calling earth-dwellers to repentance (9:20–21). These plagues are in some sense an answer to the prayers of the saints at 6:9–11—not that they ask for *them*, but for justice. They are modelled on the plagues of Egypt (Exodus 8–12), which met with similar impenitence, but led up to the final deliverance. They destroy a 'third', intensifying the 'fourth' of 6:8.

The 'great mountain' that poisons the sea is Jeremiah's term for Babylon (51:25), which is now Rome. The fallen star that poisons the waters is the king of Babylon (Isaiah 14:4, 12). '[Because they have gone after Baal...] I will feed this people with wormwood and give them poisonous water to drink' (Jeremiah 9:15). 'Wormwood is the star of the new Babylon which has poisoned by its idolatries the springs of its own life' (G.B. Caird). Environmentalists warn how in pursuit of profit and comfort we are destroying our habitat. Chernobyl is Russian for wormwood! Would the Third World have any doubt how to interpret 9:20–21?

As with the seals, the first four trumpets form a separate group. The last three, introduced by the screech of the eagle, are characterized as three *woes* (cf Ezekiel's scroll). Chapter 9 gives the first two in horrific detail. But where is the third?

3 The two witnesses *Read Revelation 10:1—11:14*

This interlude is still within the 'second woe' (11:14) and in conscious counterpoint to its impenitent outcome (11:13). For the plagues of divine wrath (not bad temper, but the recoil of sin upon the sinner which God allows) give place to the gospel. This is God's direct action, the good news of his victory and reign (Isaiah 52:7), as he announced (Greek 'evangelized') to his servants the prophets (10:7). The rainbow takes us back to 4:3, and the 'mighty angel' to the sealed scroll (5:2). Here at last we have its contents, scaled down for human consumption (10:9, 10)—sweet in its purpose (Ezekiel 3:3), but bitter in its effects (11:5–10). The sealing up of the seven thunders may be like God's mercy shortening the days of tribulation (Mark

13:20). 'Prophesy' (10:11; 11:3) means to preach the gospel, and the witnesses (two is the biblical number for witness) represent the whole church, God's living temple. Measuring (11:1), like sealing, signifies protection—inward and spiritual: externally the true church is being trampled, for the mysterious 42 months or three and half years of Daniel 12:7, which is also the time of its power. External weakness *and* spiritual power: this is the true nature of the Church.

The two witnesses reproduce the miracles of Moses and Elijah (11:5, 6), and are a torment to the idolatrous earth-dwellers (11:10). To their relief the beast from the abyss (see chapter 13) kills them in the great city (Babylon-Rome) which 'in prophetic language' (REB) is Sodom and Egypt—where also their Lord was crucified. It is Jerusalem too! As Isaiah warned, the holy city can become a harlot, its leaders and people like Sodom (1:10, 21)—a reminder that this book is addressed not to the Roman world (which would not be listening), but to the good Church members being seduced into conformity with this world.

But the eclipse of the gospel and its witnesses is followed by resurrection, sign of divine vindication. Giving glory to God is the mark of penitence; 'terrified' is better translated 'awe-struck' (11:13). It is the lived gospel, not the plagues which merely harden them, which brings people to their senses.

4 War in heaven—the third woe   *Read Revelation 11:14—12:17*

The previous section, the church's task of evangelism, was still part of the 'second woe'. Now a heavenly interlude, like that after the sixth seal, leads up to the third. The sounding of the seventh trumpet does not itself introduce a disaster. It celebrates 'Thy kingdom come', the vindication of the faithful and the destruction of the destroyers (again a warning to our First World?). First there is an enigmatic picture of the coming of Messiah. The 'woman' is another kaleidoscopic figure—Eve, Jerusalem, faithful Israel, Mary, the Church. But the reference is not to Bethlehem, Herod's fury and the flight into Egypt. Jesus comes to God's throne (12:5) only through death. The vision reduces birth, life and death to one moment (a bit like the Apostles' Creed), and the moment crystallizes an eternal conflict—note the allusion to Genesis 3:15 at 12:17, and 'the lamb slain before the foundation of the world' at 13:8.

How can there be war in heaven? Heaven can mean the pure realm of God against our mixed earth, as in the Lord's Prayer. More often it is the spiritual counterpart of this earth, containing the ambivalent sea (4:6)—and Satan himself. Michael's victory in heaven, as 12:11 shows, is just a reflection of Christ's victory on earth, carried on in his witnesses. It is a picture of 'justification' (acquittal). The throne-room is also a law court. Our accuser (12:10) is thrown out (John 12:31; Romans 8:33), thrown down to earth (Luke 10:18) to wage a bloody but ultimately futile battle against Christ's witnesses.

Here is the 'third woe' (12:12): the devil's strategy in setting up the kingdom of the 'beast', the pseudochrist (Mark 13:22). He will ascend from the abyss (where over-confident Christians thought he was safely tied up, perhaps following Mark 3:27?), and the visionary fate of the two witnesses (11:8) will become a terrible reality. But the Church as temple (11:1–2) and mother (12:13–17), though outwardly under attack, is still inwardly under divine protection.

5 The two beasts *Read Revelation 13*

The beast from the sea is a composite of the four beasts of Daniel 7, which represent world empires: all arrogance and bullying of God's people is now concentrated in Rome and its divine emperor. This, the focus of the world's admiration and worship (13:3, 4, 8, 12), is the 'third woe', its supreme disaster (14:9–11). The mortal wound healed could refer to Nero, who had massacred Christians in Rome in the sixties. He had died in mysterious circumstances; soon a rumour arose that he was alive and would come with an avenging army from the East. Later this became a demonic Nero with an army from hell. Or it could refer to the Roman Empire, on the verge of collapse in the civil wars that followed Nero's death, but resurrected under Vespasian and his sons, Titus and Domitian. On another level it is a parody of the true Christ's death and resurrection.

The beast's blasphemies are against God's 'dwelling', which is people not a place (see on 11:1–2). Those who dwell in heaven are not in this case angels, but those whose treasure is in heaven—over against the earth-dwellers, whose treasure and horizons are earth-bound (in verse 8 follow REB, not RSV. The Greek runs '... the lamb slain before the foundation of the world'). 'If anyone has an ear' is a reminder to conforming Christians of the warnings in chapters 2 and 3. Verse 10, alluding to Jeremiah 15:2, warns that the fate of the witnesses is not to be evaded—nor is the beast to be fought with his own weapons (Matthew 26:51–56).

If the sea-beast is a parody of Christ, then the second beast is a parody of the Holy Spirit. Its 'signs' and 'fire from heaven' are a parody of the Pentecostal fire and apostolic miracles (cf Mark 13:22). It comes from the land—probably the local protagonists of the emperor cult—and looks like a lamb, that is, it takes in even Christians. Political and economic pressure would work together with texts like Romans 13, which led German Christians to go along with Hitler, and South African Christians with apartheid.

666: the ancients were fascinated by numbers. Each letter of the alphabet had numerical value (there were no Arabic numerals), so a name could be added up, and a number could hide a name. The call for 'wisdom' is not for skill in guessing; there is evidence that 666 was already a code for Nero. It is rather a call for discernment, to see that the good emperor, hailed as Benefactor, Saviour, Son of God, in fact reincarnates the monster Nero—no doubt a shock for patriotic citizens, as if one had made such a suggestion about Mrs Thatcher. In apocalyptic we are in the realm of political cartoons and *Private Eye*. Symbolically, 6 is one short of 7, the number of perfection. It is thus the number of antichrist. Satan was the highest of the angels, but the almost perfect claiming perfection, the penultimate claiming ultimacy, is the very devil.

6 The winepress of God's wrath *Read Revelation 14*

Satan stood on the sand (12:17). The Lamb stands on the rock of Zion (cf Matthew 7:24–27?). Over against those with the name and number of the beast on their foreheads stand the 144,000, with the name of the Lamb and his father (the baptismal seal) on theirs. Verse 4 is one of the most misunderstood in the Bible. Just as fornication is a metaphor for spiritual infidelity, so is chastity (the Greek has 'for they are virgins') for spiritual dedication. The point is not abstinence from sex but total dedication. In Israel soldiers and priests abstained while on duty—the 144,000 are spiritually both (5:10). The first fruits of the harvest represent the whole (cf 1 Corinthians 15:20).

The angel flying in midheaven is a counterpart of the woe-angel of 8:13. The gospel is the good news of God's victory, and so a challenge to those who worship false gods. It is victory over Babylon, the source of intoxication—no good drying out the alcoholic without cutting off the source of supply! The terrible picture of the unresting torment of false worship is a caricature of the unresting worship of heaven (4:8). It is a picture of what will happen if people continue on that track, in order that it may not happen, a call for faithful endurance.

Like the seals series, the trumpets series builds up to a picture of the End, here in terms of harvest and vintage drawn from Joel 3:13. John brings in the ghastly picture of God trampling the blood of his enemies as in a wine press from Isaiah 63:1–6. The Targum, the Aramaic paraphrase read in the synagogue after the Hebrew, linked this passage with Genesis 49:9–11, the lion of Judah. If John reinterpreted that (5:5–6), must he not have reinterpreted this likewise? In fact 'outside the city' was a pointer to the cross (Hebrews 13:12; cf Luke 4:29; 20:15) and martyrdom (Acts 7:58). God's vengeance takes not the blood of his enemies but the blood of his own.

GUIDELINES

In Revelation we have a 'rebirth of images'. It encourages us to reread all scripture, especially the violent and vindictive passages, in the light of Christ crucified, the slain Lamb. It requires mental gymnastics as we read, and moral gymnastics as we try to live it; it needs long practice. John, we may feel, has not himself got very far; there is an element of caricature and savagery in his treatment of opposition. In a situation of injustice and false religion, addressed to the complacent, such language may be necessary; the 'testimony of Jesus' is not just turning the other cheek. But outside such a situation it is different; violence begets violence. Even in the old South Africa the spirited gentleness and humour of a Steve Biko or a Desmond Tutu was perhaps more lamb-like, and ultimately more effective.

Almighty God, who hast given thy only Son to be unto us both a sacrifice for sin, and also an example of godly life; give us grace that we may always most thankfully receive that his inestimable benefit, and also daily endeavour ourselves to follow the blessed steps of his most holy life; through the same Jesus Christ our Lord.

The Collect for the second Sunday after Easter

M·

1   The bowls of wrath   *Read Revelation 15 and 16*

The trumpet plagues are aimed primarily at the beast, the emperor; this series targets his city, Rome, and its grip on the world's resources. The removal of this grip leads to the world's fulfilment; it is not, as might seem, a case of flood-like extermination. Admittedly, these plagues end in total impenitence (16:9–11, 21), like the trumpet plagues (9:20–1), and the Exodus plagues which are the model for both. But they are introduced by a song which celebrates a new and greater exodus. The sea of 4:6 has now become the Red Sea, and the triumph song of Moses (Exodus 15: 'the Lord is a man of war') becomes the song of the Lamb, drawing on one of the few universalistic Psalms (86:9). It is the same 'rebirth of images' as with lion and lamb.

The 'bowls of wrath' come from one of the four living creatures (15:7). 'Wrath' is sin recoiling upon the sinner, nature taking its revenge (cf Judges 5:19–21), but it is not just natural nemesis. It stems from the temple, from God's presence. It is his 'strange work', in Luther's phrase. His 'proper work' is different, but for the moment justice must be done (16:5–7). Note 'thou who art and wast': no 'to come'. This is final.

The fifth bowl moves from nature to the city, the beast's throne, which people were getting too friendly with at Pergamum (2:13–15). The sixth strikes the Euphrates, the historic starting point for invasion from the East, and Christ's interjection at verse 15 is a pointed reminder of sleepy Sardis (3:1–3). These visions are less to comfort the afflicted, in Desmond Tutu's words, than to afflict the comfortable.

Armageddon (verse 16) has caused endless speculation. It was perhaps a commonplace at the time, but became a riddle, like 666 and much of Revelation's imagery which baffles us. It means in Hebrew 'mountain of Meggido', a famous battlefield, where the stars in their courses fought for Israel (Judges 5:19–21 again). The nearest mountain was Carmel, where Elijah met the prophets of Baal (1 Kings 18:19ff.) in the time of Ahab and Jezebel.

Finally, the great city falls, and all its satellites. Unlike the earthquake at 11:13 this one does not lead to penitence. But 11:8 told us that the great city is also Jerusalem, where the Lord was crucified, for the sin of the world (John 1:29). The prostitute bride is never beyond her husband's strategy for redemption (Hosea 1–3).

2 The fall of the great whore *Read Revelation 17:1–14; 18:9–20*

These two chapters are more Moses than Lamb, but wait for 21:9, which pointedly picks up 17:1. Now the angel carries John into a wilderness. Biblical geography, like its arithmetic, is symbolic and ambivalent: the desert was the place of Israel's honeymoon with God (Jeremiah 2:2) and of idolatry and fornication (the golden calf). For Jesus it was the place of temptation, but also of vision, seeing through the attractions of worldly solutions. So here this beautifully attired woman (notice the echo of the true mother at 12:1) is shown to be the ruthless mother of all deception and dirt. But John is still dazzled (17:6), like the earth-dwellers (13:4) and Christian fellow-travellers. Rome was immensely powerful, beautiful and superficially beneficial, its bestial past forgotten. The beast 'was and is not' (17:8), but is soon to emerge and mobilize the 'ten kings' (17:12ff.), the hostile powers latent on the empire's borders, and destroy it. (This happened— eventually; another case of a line reduced to a point by perspective!)

Much ingenuity has been spent identifying the emperors referred to, but seven is the number of completeness, and John probably means the series of emperors as a whole. The point is that he and his hearers are at the penultimate stage, the sinister sixth, a time of apparent security, when they have never had it so good. But the beast is about to appear, in true Nero colours.

We turn now to the lament of the other 'kings'—her clients (18:9ff.; the chapter begins with a chain of allusions to the fall of Babylon in the prophets). In the ancient world all wealth, power and patronage was in the hands of a tiny élite, who built a brilliant and luxurious civilization on a base of conquest, asset-stripping and slave labour (not totally different from the British Empire in the eighteenth and nineteenth centuries). Notice the decline of value of the articles listed in verses 12–13: jewels, silks, metal work, spices, ordinary food-stuffs, animals, vehicles, and at the bottom of the heap, translating literally, 'bodies, that is, human souls'. 'Bodies' was a word for slaves, like 'hands' for workers. It is an indictment the more telling for its restraint. Does it not apply to any society where workers are exploited and profit is the bottom line?

3 The marriage supper of the Lamb
Read Revelation 18:20—19:21

Jeremiah was told to throw a stone into the Euphrates, and say 'Thus shall Babylon sink, to rise no more' (51:63–64). John makes it a 'great millstone' (Matthew 18:6) and thus widens the application to all who make little ones 'stumble', like the Nicolaitans (2:14). Likewise 'sorcery' (18:23) was a mark of Jezebel (2:20; 2 Kings 9:22). Witchcraft, like astrology, dominated people's minds: Ephesus was a centre of magic (Acts 19:18–19). We today might think of the hold of advertising and the media, and secret systems of surveillance and control.

The final removal of this incubus heralds the V Day celebrations, based on the Hallel Psalms (113–118), which celebrated the Passover deliverance. 'Praise our God' (19:5) is Hallelujah! in Greek. It culminates in the marriage supper of the Lamb (of which the Lord's supper was a foretaste). The sleeping bride is now awake, and ready— the nakedness of Laodicea and the soiled garments of Sardis left behind. The faithful lives of her members are her adornment.

Now follows what Christians looked forward to as Christ's Parousia, or Coming—not that he was absent; it was to be the manifestation of his hidden victory for every eye to see (1:7). There are echoes of the opening vision and messages—and of the wine press of 14:20. Notice that his robe is dipped in blood before he treads it. It is not the blood of his enemies; his sword is the word of truth, piercing our delusions. Finally, there is the ghastly parody of the supper of the Lamb, in language drawn mainly from Ezekiel 39:4, 17–20. The best one can say is that it is meant to shock the complacent; the ugliness of the language bodies out the ugliness of idolatry and its end product, over against the beauty of holiness.

4 The millennium and the Lamb's book of life
Read Revelation 20

It is odd that the millennium has so exercised imaginations. It is a tiny section of John's visionary canvas, and, like so much of his material, it is part of the apocalyptic stock in trade. God's final coming to redress this wicked earth is not a job for an afternoon. From one perspective the line can be reduced to a point, like Paul's 'twinkling of an eye' (1 Corinthians 15:52), but transforming human hearts and wills must be a line, a process. So the Jews envisaged an interim, a period of education under the messianic king—40 years, or 400 (as in 2 Esdras 7:28ff.), or 1000, which was reckoned to be the proper span of life before the Fall. It's a time of preparing for the new heaven and earth, like astronauts practising for the moon.

But why the final unbinding of Satan, and rebellion of Gog and Magog? It comes from Ezekiel 38–39, which emphasizes that the victims of this attack 'dwell securely' (38:8, 11, 14; 39:26). Under the conditions of this heaven and earth, with human free will not yet properly aligned with God's, Satan has a necessary place. He vividly symbolizes that our freedom is genuine, no divine manipulation behind the scenes, and that complacency, as in the Asian churches, is a constant danger. Poor Satan, then, 'tormented day and night for ever and ever'? No wonder some have thought Satan the hero (like Prometheus in Greek mythology) and God the devil! But the Satanic trinity are an abstraction, and 'eternal torture' is rhetoric, to express the seriousness of present choices (cf Matthew 13:42, 50; 18:34; 25:46).

The books of judgment (verse 12) are again part of the stock in trade. We are judged by the account books of our deeds, but the last word is with the 'other book', the book of life of the Lamb slain before the foundation of the world (13:8). In the Bible free will and predestination stand side by side. There are earth-dwellers 'whose names have not been written in the book of life from the foundation of the world' (17:8), but it cannot be literal predestination because the earth-dwellers are called to repent, and names written in the book can be blotted out (3:5). The Bible sets side by side God's determination to save from eternity, and our freedom to refuse. There can be no complacency. But, for faith, can there be doubt who will win?

5 **The new heaven and the new earth**
   Read Revelation 21:1—22:5

We can see the need for a new earth, but why a new heaven? Why no more sea? The answer lies back in chapter 4. Heaven can be God's abode in contrast with earth, but it can also be the spiritual realm behind the visible creation and therefore equally open to disorder and rebellion. The sea and Satan, both dragons, have their place in heaven, until God's plan is completed. In the old heaven and earth it is possible not to sin; in the new it is not possible to sin. Human wills are at last freely aligned with God's; he has fulfilled the hope which the feast of Tabernacles symbolized of God dwelling with his people, as he did after the Exodus (21:3–4, echoing 7:9–17). But the dwelling is not now in tents, but in a city wholly dedicated to God, as a bride to her husband.

The same bowl-angel who showed John the judgment of the harlot-city now shows him the bride, but what is the relation between the two? Simply demolition and replacement? Has God forgotten his promise to Noah, and, since the city is also Jerusalem (11:8), his promises to Israel? That is no doubt what many Christians, then and since, have thought. But the kings of the earth, who, like the great city, have been gruesomely destroyed, are bringing in their glory (21:24); the leaves of the tree (*xulon*, the cross; 1 Peter 2:24 etc.) are for the healing of the nations, and the curse of Genesis 3 is undone (22:2, 3). We already have the key in Lion and Lamb: it is not scrapping but transfiguration, and the secret of the alchemy is the fidelity and purity of the Lamb and his witnesses. The bride's fine linen is the righteous deeds of the saints (19:8).

There is no space to expound the city's details; enough to note the ubiquity of 12 (salvation *is* from the Jews), the beauty of the jewels (to the ear, rather than the eye; we do not know exactly what many of them are), and the dimensions. The city is not just foursquare; it is a cube (21:16)—the shape of the Holy of Holies in Solomon's temple, where only the High Priest could enter, on the Day of Atonement. The city has no temple, because it is all temple, all Holy of Holies. All are one with God and the Lamb for ever, absorbed in worship, like Charles Wesley's worshippers 'lost in wonder, love and praise'.

6 *Marana tha*—Come, Lord Jesus   *Read Revelation 22:6–21*

John's book began like a Pauline letter, and ends like one with a string of messages and warnings underlining the main thrust, and leading into the eucharist—the occasion when such letters would be read out. 'Coming soon' picks up 1:1–3 and the messages to the churches. Christians did at first look forward to Christ's coming very soon, and perhaps to a messianic kingdom like the millennium (cf Matthew 19:28; Luke 22:30). But by the end of the century they turned more to Jesus' own confession of ignorance about the Day (Mark 13:32). At about the time of Revelation, probably, Luke was writing his Gospel, with Jesus' warning. 'Take heed that you are not led astray; for many will come in my name saying... "The time is at hand"... but the end will not be at once.' Many in Asia may have seen John as such a false prophet.

In fact the New Testament holds together both the long haul, the journey through the desert, and the vivid expectancy that the End of all things, which (or rather who) has already come, may break in at any moment. Paul saw Christ's coming in the eucharist as a powerful anticipation of his final Coming, which must mean judgment—danger for those unprepared (1 Corinthians 11:26–32). The letter ends with the exclusion of anyone who does not love the Lord—*Marana tha* (Come, Lord). John likewise ends as if the die is already cast (vv. 10–11). But verse 14 calls us to renew our baptismal dedication; the sense is 'blessed are those who keep washing their clothes'. Baptism is both a once for all point (the seal, 7:2–3), and a line, a journey. We already belong in the city, but must enter (keep entering) by the gates. Each gate is a pearl, which reminds us that entering the kingdom costs all we have and are (Matthew 13:46). All enslaved to falsehood are necessarily outside. Whether there will be any such in the end is not for us to say. Our part is simply to come, and receive the One who is always coming to us. Even so, come Lord Jesus!

GUIDELINES

Revelation is full of eucharistic imagery which is deeply meaningful to most Christians. The baptismal imagery is equally strong, but perhaps less central for us, especially those baptized in infancy. Baptism does, however, marvellously crystallize the heart of the gospel: God's unmerited love and acceptance of us in Christ; his dying to loose us from our sins, calling us into his death from sin to live for God. His seal on our foreheads is the antidote to the mark of the beast, on those whose horizons are bounded by this world. Certainly we cannot presume on our baptism, as if we had already arrived, like some at Corinth (1 Corinthians 4:8), and in the Asian churches. But we can and should rejoice in it, take confidence from it on our desert journey, and celebrate its anniversary, for ourselves, our children and godchildren, even more than our natural birthdays.

Almighty God, we thank you for our fellowship in the household of faith with all those who have been baptized in your name. Keep us faithful to our baptism, and so make us ready for that day when the whole creation shall be made perfect in your Son, our Saviour Jesus Christ.

For further reading

G.B. Caird, *The Revelation of St John the Divine*, A. & C. Black, 1966

J.-P. Prévost, *How to Read the Apocalypse*, SCM Press, 1993

C.C. Rowland, *Revelation*, Epworth, 1993

J.P.M. Sweet, *Revelation*, SCM Press, 1979 and 1990

Hosea

The opening chapters of Hosea (1–3) introduce us to a prophet whose message is closely bound up with his personal life, and though the overall picture is clear the details are not. What is clear is that Hosea married a wife, Gomer, who was either a prostitute at the time of the marriage or who became a prostitute afterwards. By some it has been suggested that she proved 'an unfaithful wife' and by others that she was a temple prostitute when Hosea married her, though we cannot be sure that such prostitutes existed in Hosea's time and if they did we know very little about them. They may have been part of ancient Canaanite fertility rituals which Israel had tried to avoid. What is also clear is that Hosea remained faithful to her and loved her throughout. By some it has been suggested that this was because Hosea believed he ought to treat her as Yahweh had treated Israel and by others that it was through his own personal experience that he came to a new appreciation of Yahweh's love for his people. Perhaps we do not have to choose and there is value in a fluidity of thought and imagination as Hosea encountered both experiences simultaneously.

Because this is not only the most human part of the book but also the most readily understood, it is not difficult to convince ourselves that we know what Hosea's message is about—a loving God who has no illusions about the faithlessness of his partner, who is constantly hurt by her behaviour and not infrequently angry with her attitudes, yet who loves her so much for her own sake that he can never cast her off. It is not a bad summary and possibly an important message which we all need to hear, but chapters 1–3 are not necessarily the best place to begin studying the book for two reasons.

First, it makes it too easy to overlook those aspects of Hosea's message which do not relate directly to his marriage. His prophecy, for example, is to the community rather than individuals and therefore it is a limitation to begin with the personal. Better first to appreciate our common plight (namely, the nature and extent of our failure) so as to feel the wonder of God's love even more.

Secondly, Hosea's marriage needs to be seen in the light of his message, not vice versa. It is easy to think we understand what is meant by prostitution and from that to infer what Yahweh (and Hosea) are saying of Israel, but it would be better first to grasp the heart of what they are saying and then, if it looks like 'prostitution', try to appreciate what Yahweh does with 'prostitutes' through the experience of Hosea with Gomer. The first method encourages us to identify with the righteous and feel revulsion for the wicked; the second may enable us to see the failure in ourselves and then to feel the essence of forgiveness.

This is why we begin with chapter 4. Readers who want the background should read 2 Kings 14:23—18:12. Remember that Hosea is not an easy book. The Hebrew text is not very clear, hence the variations in translation. Avoid getting bogged down in detail and try rather to grasp the overall message.

References will be to The New Revised Standard Version.

21–27 APRIL   WHAT IS WRONG

1   Judgment on the community   *Read Hosea 4:1–14*

We are in the law courts. Yahweh's case against Israel is clear and straightforward. What is lacking is a knowledge of God. The evidence is mixed. There is direct disobedience—the commandments are being broken. There are side-effects—violence is one sign of an unhappy society. And the effects are far-reaching—the desolation of the land and the failure of animals and fish suggest we are not just talking about minor, incidental or personal peccadilloes. We have a problem of community. All nature is groaning under the strain and the people know it. They feel it every day.

Who then is responsible? The prime responsibility has to be carried by the priests and prophets, partly because it is their job to create and maintain a fair and healthy society and partly because if they themselves are lacking in a knowledge of God what hope is there for the rest? So, 'whom the Lord loveth he chasteneth' and just as Jesus reserved his severest strictures for the Pharisees, who in all Judaism were nearest to him in approach and attitude but who still showed signs of self-interest, so Hosea's word is directed initially against those from whom most might reasonably have been expected.

Their offence? To say it is immorality or idolatry may be too easy, though there is no lack of evidence (v. 14). Closer reading of the text, however, suggests it is putting their own interests before the needs of others—feeding on the people (v. 8)—and resorting either to the popular cults of the day (v. 12) or to the worship patterns of yesterday (v. 13) whilst at the same time forgetting the *true* meaning of 'yesterday'—Yahweh's deliverance of them from Egypt.

And the result? People are still going through the motions—evil as well as good—but they are finding no meaning or satisfaction in them (v. 10) and the community is falling apart. But they are not to blame other people. The leaders may be irresponsible but the judgement is on the people.

2 A word for the leaders   *Read Hosea 5:1–7*

This is a joint attack on both the religious and political leaders more by allusion than by direct speech. Hosea wants to touch their hearts and consciences rather than argue with their minds. Hosea and his hearers know that they have sinned before and they will sin again, but they also know that things were not always like this. Perhaps their memories need a jog!

Shittim was the last encampment of the Israelites *en route* from Egypt to Canaan and as such had a special significance, but the very mention of it was also sufficient to remind them that it was traditionally the place where they first succumbed to immorality and idolatry (Numbers 25). Tabor and Mizpah, similarly, were once sacred shrines but now they too had become defiled. To feel the force of the prophecy try recalling three similar sites or events in your own national history.

Then, to the imaginary riposte that 'it's all you can expect from places and people like that', Hosea proceeds to point out that even for favourites like Ephraim (Israel) and Judah the record is no better. Even those who had received special care and attention and those in whom Yahweh had most hope have failed him also. There is no escape from our own responsibilities and failings by drawing attention to the failures of others, though the temptation is never far away; all Yahweh does is to invite us to look in a mirror.

And Hosea implies that because it is all so obvious they cannot help but be aware of it. They must know 'it isn't working any more'— they are going through the motions but they are deriving neither results nor satisfaction. Why? Because God has withdrawn from them—or because their manner of life has created such a gulf between them and Yahweh that not even he will bridge it (but see v. 15).

3 Hosea's exasperation   *Read Hosea 6:1–11*

The change of mood between verses 3 and 4 reveals something of Hosea's frustration, caught between the good intentions of the people (vv. 1–3) and the enduring love of Yahweh for his people (v. 4). But can we see it also as a reflection of Yahweh's frustration? On the surface, hurt and disappointment in a loving relationship which he would love to overcome by cool rationality (cf Isaiah 1:13), balanced by the irritation that boils up (v. 4) and the judgment that takes over (v. 5). It is the experience of many a loving parent when faced by the transitoriness and uncertainty (the 'dew' or the 'morning cloud' of v. 4) of an unstable adolescent.

But even in moments of the coolest rationality are they really being rational? Or are they retreating into rationality to escape from an impossible situation by harbouring expectations which, though reasonable, may be totally inappropriate? If, as seems to be the case (vv. 7–10), the ruling élite and the people have created a society in which wickedness no longer seems to matter (so that either there is robbery on the streets with the priests into it as much as anybody else or there is a priesthood up to its neck in greed as much as street robbers) and if the official line seems to be that there is nothing here that cannot be put right by a few religious rites and ceremonies (sacrifice and burnt offerings, v. 6), then maybe they have to understand that something much more radical is called for.

What Yahweh is looking for is what Yahweh has already given— 'steadfast love' (v. 6). *Hesed* is a difficult word to translate—sometimes 'lovingkindness', sometimes 'tender mercy'. Consult a variety of translations to plumb its depth. But then remember that it is a word which sums up everything God is prepared to do for us and consider how he longs for nothing less in return. So how can we show that same 'steadfast love' for him?

4 More stupid than wicked?   *Read Hosea 7:1–16*

Could it be that these people are not so much inherently wicked as plain stupid—a 'silly dove' (v. 11)? If so, in what does their stupidity consist? Hosea gives several hints.

First, they appear to be more interested in living with their problems (v. 1) than in asking questions about causes or trying to make changes and so pre-empt disaster. They run away from consequences rather than face them and search for explanations. Moreover, they seem quite oblivious to the fact that Yahweh knows full well what is going on; in other words, that there is an ultimate authority to which they must give account.

Secondly, they are more interested in pleasing their masters (kings and officials) than they are in pleasing Yahweh by doing what is right. Long-term goodness may be sacrificed for short-term gain. The oven metaphor seems to suggest that far from 'trying to please' they are in fact in a situation which has got totally out of control. They are little more than puppets on a string!

Thirdly, how stupid can you get when you obviously need no encouragement to turn to kings, all of whom have let you down, yet refuse to call upon Yahweh who never has (v. 7)?

Well, stupidity, no less than weakness and outright sinfulness, brings its own reward. Those who live by plotting will die by plotting, only this time it will be Yahweh who is in charge. But if they are indeed as Hosea describes will they ever understand what brought them down any more than they have understood who was their 'Maker' (8:14)?

5 How dare you celebrate? *Read Hosea 9:1–12*

Imagine these words being uttered by the prophet at a festival as he contemplates the revelry, the eating and the drinking, and reflects on the state of the nation. This was a society in which the sacred and the secular were often indistinguishable. The threshing floor and the wine presses that produced the bread and the wine for pleasure and sustenance produced it for worship also, much as in Western society church buildings, the use of Sunday, rites of passage and even the sacraments can cross the barriers of the sacred and the secular to provide a service to both.

Their offence here was that their blindness (or self-confidence) had led them to imagine that it all belonged to them and they could do with it as they liked, with the result that they had reduced something which was always secular and potentially sacred to the level of a bare necessity—'for their hunger only' (v. 4, cf 1 Corinthians 11:20–22). This was more than the breaking of a commandment, for what had been so abused could no longer fulfil its holy purpose. The vehicle for the spiritual had been destroyed and once that damage has been done it is very difficult to repair it. Here we have the essence of 'prostitution' which goes much wider than sexual relationships.

This time they have gone too far, says the prophet; even if they change course now Egypt will either destroy them or make life very uncomfortable (v. 6). The reference to Gibeah is to the horrific story in Judges 19, a particularly dark patch in their history when there was no king because 'every man did that which was right in his own eyes'. It is as if they were returning to Egypt—to slavery—to the level and attitudes from which Yahweh had delivered their fathers when he found them 'like grapes in the desert' (v. 10). No wonder they try to dismiss Hosea as a fool (v. 7) but Hosea knows that you don't annul the message by shooting the messenger.

6 Nothing but talk *Read Hosea 10:1–8*

Israel is a people which has risen from nothing and known prosperity ('a luxuriant vine', v. 1) but a careful observer like Hosea could not miss the fact that in recent years the people have lost their soul. Having found their God (or having been found by him) in slavery, they too quickly lost him once they secured their freedom. All that remains is a shell. Everything is still in place and the right things are still being said but the heart has gone out of it. Sacrifice and ritual are honoured more than meaningful and loving relationships. Altars to false gods have multiplied (v. 1) but the obligations of personal relationships, whether to a king or to the Lord, no longer seem to matter (v. 3).

With loss of faith has also gone the loss of the social graces within the community. Litigation increased as people were increasingly unable to trust one another to speak the truth and to deal fairly (v. 4). When their misdeeds come to light they run for cover and use all means to avoid being found out (v. 8). 'Beth-aven' (v. 5) means 'House of Wickedness', an ironical renaming of Bethel, House of God. The calf image of Bethel, the object of their worship, is to the prophet merely 'the thing', a helpless artifact (v. 6).

At one level this is the gap between ritual and reality, sometimes expressed by those people who believe that if your heart is in the right place all rituals are unnecessary. At another level it is the gap between (a) ritual that is *expressive* of something meaningful and (b) ritual that is a *substitute* for something meaningful. In the latter case the ritual is all that is left.

GUIDELINES

One way to appreciate the relevance of Hosea's word for our own society today is to ask two important questions of the text.

- *Which 'bits' of Hosea's charge against the community of his day might apply equally to our society? Once you have taken the text in its most literal form (e.g. they had prostitution, we have prostitution) try to explore different levels. Identify different kinds of 'prostitution' and idolatry in your everyday world and face the challenge.*

- *Which 'bits' of our society need to hear Hosea's message today, and why? Who is most likely to hear it? With whom is it most unlikely to be popular?*

You might re-read one or two verses which 'spoke' to you particularly and write down what they said. Then look at some of the verses again to see what you were not 'hearing'.

---

28 APRIL–4 MAY WHAT IS NEEDED TO PUT IT RIGHT

1 Yahweh's dilemma *Read Hosea 11:1–9*

The prophet portrays Yahweh in human terms, a loving parent of a wayward child, baffled by the way his people behave. After all he has done (vv. 3–4) he finds himself rejected (v. 2). Did Hosea's contemporaries, like so many of us, take things for granted and never really stop to pause and consider where they came from? How had they got where they were? Whose vision and direction made it possible? Who rescued them when they were in trouble and who loved them when they were desperate for reassurance? Yet not only do they fail to respond to him but half the time they are rushing off in the opposite direction.

But then the next minute Yahweh himself is in a different mood, reflecting, prophetically and remorsefully, on what is happening, or is going to happen to them if they don't mend their ways, and even contemplating certain punishments to mete out to them (vv. 5–7), only to swing back at verses 8–9 with the realization that in no way can he let them down or give them up (Admah and Zeboiim are closely linked with Sodom and Gomorrah, see Genesis 10:19; 13:10).

149

Perhaps we see here shades of Hosea wrestling with his own relationship with Gomer. How can he continue to love her as she is? But then how can give her up? And what other alternative has he got? Perhaps he needs to change his attitude or mood, as Yahweh did, from love to rejection and back again. But how? Read again the beginning of the chapter. Re-establish in your mind that picture of a loving parent/child relationship for here is a clue. Yet the forgiveness of verse 9 is not inevitable. It is superhuman love; 'I am God', says Yahweh, 'not a man.' And the God who can transform personal relationships can transform nations too. This way lies the road to healing.

2   Israel's Treachery   *Read Hosea 12:1–14*

Before Yahweh his people stand wrong-footed on all counts. To the charge that 'things today are a lot worse than they used to be' the prophet reminds them in no uncertain terms that they had been pretty bad from the beginning (vv. 3–4). The struggle between Jacob and Esau in the womb (Genesis 25:22) is symptomatic of a continual struggle for supremacy (Genesis 32:24ff).

To those on the other hand who find comfort in the idea that 'things have always been like this' (vv. 7–8) the prophet agrees but goes on to add 'yes... and look what happened' (v. 9).

And to those who are thinking 'well, you would expect a prophet to behave like that' or 'don't take too much notice, it's only the prophet saying that' he is careful to point out that the one who stands behind the prophets and speaks through them is none other than Yahweh himself (v. 10). The prophets have been at the heart of Israel's faith and existence from the beginning (v. 13) and both Gilead and Gilgal testify to what happens when the prophets are not heard. The Gilead reference (v. 11) may be to the time when fifty of them were engaged in revolutionary activity (2 Kings 15:25ff) or to the occasion later when they were carried off into Assyria (v. 29), and Gilgal (v. 11) was an ancient sanctuary whose dubious sacrificial practices had brought about a decline in favour of Jerusalem.

Two points ought not to be missed. First, the real offence is not so much wickedness as arrogance (*hybris*) which not only fails to notice the damage which their behaviour is causing but actually glories in it to the point of calling it success (v. 8). It is not difficult to recognize this in others or in society as a whole but it is very easy to miss it in ourselves. But secondly, with Yahweh there is always the possibility of forgiveness provided there is repentance. Yet he is not a God to be trifled with: 'The Lord is his name!' (vv. 5–6).

3 Sentence of death   *Read Hosea 13:4–16*

This is a fearsome passage. Just as the drama seems to be playing itself out nicely along the lines of repentance, forgiveness and restoration there is yet one more twist in the tail—there is talk of judgment, for sin is serious. The words are uncompromising: 'compassion is hidden from my eyes' (v. 14). You can almost feel Yahweh's wrestling to avoid the inevitable sentence of death.

First, he agonizes over the relationship (vv. 4–6). It was so close. And for so long. Not only the exodus but the continual care ever since, first in the wilderness, then in the settlement. These statements are not only fact but also symbols. Surely they must remember the miracle of the manna—and the rock. Had he not remained faithful 'through all the changing scenes of life'? How could they have forgotten! Yet even so, much more hurtful than anything anybody has done is the breaking of the relationship, particularly when the break was not so much the result of a quarrel as of indifference. Fences really do have to be mended—between Yahweh and his people, between Hosea and Gomer, and of course between all his people, now as then.

Secondly, do they remember the ones who have exploited them more than those who have loved them—the bear and the leopard in the wilderness as against Yahweh who fed them (vv. 7–8)? Maybe there is here even a touch of tragic humour. Israel's enemies were sometimes portrayed as wild animals. Is Yahweh suggesting that if he really wants their response perhaps he ought to try exploiting them instead of loving them for it is often the case that we are drawn most to those who exploit us and respond least to those who love us most?

But then thirdly, the harshest of all. Should he hand them over to death? Or can he treat them as they have treated him? Can he too forget and leave them to self-destruction through their military exploits? God's remedy is radical. The impasse is broken, as we shall see in the following reading.

4 Yahweh cannot give up those he loves   *Read Hosea 14:1–8*

Yahweh can neither hand them over to death nor can he forget them. But no more can he carry on as if nothing had gone wrong. Two final acts, both of which throw light on what is needed in the relationship between Hosea and Gomer, are needed to restore Yahweh's relationship with his people.

The first is an act of genuine repentance on the part of the people. So crucial is it to Hosea that he virtually writes it for them, and it is not clear whether he writes this from the depths of his own feelings for Gomer or whether it is in composing it that he sees new possibilities for his own marriage. Nor does it matter. Better to see them as parallel situations 'talking' to each other, bringing enlightenment to each other, and then reflect on how they bring enlightenment to us today. The content of the repentance is clear. They are to put aside all feelings of guilt, turn their words into actions (v. 2), acknowledge that the way they have been living just will not work, and rely on God's mercy as if they were orphans (v. 3). The price is high, but without it there can be no forgiveness.

The second is an act of generous forgiveness on the part of Yahweh. This also is costly. It is more than words. The fact that he loves them 'freely' (v. 4) must not blind them to the solemnity of his anger or the hurt in the heart of God.

As you reflect on the feelings of Yahweh and his people as they work out their new relationship try to imagine the sort of conversations which Hosea and Gomer might have been having also.

5 The cost of suffering love   *Read Hosea 1:1–9; 3:1–5*

It is not clear whether Hosea married a whore to demonstrate his love for her and Yahweh's unfailing love for Israel, or whether he married a respectable woman who became a whore and to whom Hosea remained faithful to demonstrate Yahweh's faithfulness to Israel. It is even possible that chapters 1 and 3 refer to two different women. Some writers have suggested that it was no normal relationship but an act of prophetic symbolism whereby the prophet demonstrates his message by his action and then his action seeks to achieve that which he proclaims. Nor is it clear whether it was Hosea's experience that led him to insights about Yahweh or vice versa. The arguments will continue but need not affect our appreciation of the message. Perhaps not even Hosea could have answered the question. Maybe he never even asked it. What is clear is that in both cases the outcome was not quite what the people of that day would have expected. So how did it come about?

Possibly, as with Job, it was the result of personal experience. It could well have been a consequence of the clash between Hosea's personal experience and society's conventions. He discovered that he could no longer square his own feelings of love for Gomer with what he knew was expected of him. Yahweh, too, does the unexpected. Here we have theology built on personal experience challenging established practice, and taking risks—for love is vulnerable. It risks rejection, unpopularity and scorn. 'Love cannot help becoming hope' (Kazoh Kitamori, a Japanese theologian).

By the time Hosea has come to terms with Yahweh's enduring love for Israel (11:8) he not only has a new conviction about how he is to treat Gomer but also a new source of strength. It may not make it any easier to achieve and the old scorn and unpopularity may never go away, but at least now he knows why he is behaving as he does and in whose footsteps he is treading.

6 Love unfailing and true   Read Hosea 2

Chapter 2 moves all the time on two planes, the personal and the national, and though there is something to be said for sorting them out there is also something to be said for allowing them to flow together whilst concentrating on the underlying issues common to both. The beginning, for example, is personal, with Hosea using his children to plead on his behalf with their mother, but by the time we get to verses 9ff the picture has changed to Israel. Two issues, however, are common to both situations and are the marks of true love.

First, there is an acceptance of reality. Verses 1–13 leave us in no doubt that Hosea (Yahweh) is affronted (if not outraged) and offended (if not heart-broken) by what Gomer (Israel) has done. Nor is there any attempt to conceal his anger and desire for punishment if not revenge. Love begins, though does not end, with an acceptance of the reality of the situation in all its horror.

Secondly, there is a determination to redeem the situation. Something which has gone so dreadfully wrong must be put right. People who have grown so far apart must somehow be brought back together again. A situation which has strayed so far must be brought back to where it started. Yet whereas we tend to assume this requires a 'nevertheless' ('these people may have gone far astray, *nevertheless* it is my job to try to bring them back and forgive them') Hosea, following what he knows of Yahweh, sees it as a 'therefore' (v. 14). Both Hosea and Yahweh woo the one who has let them down, not because it is right and they feel they ought, but because love transcends sin and sorrow and they cannot help themselves.

To love is to enter into relationship—in Yahweh's case a covenantal relationship—and in that relationship we have to wrestle with that love in order to be true to ourselves. We *therefore* forgive, not 'in spite of ourselves' but 'because of ourselves'—not because it is our duty but because failure and indifference move us to go on loving.

GUIDELINES

This week we have been thinking about relationships and what has to be done when they go wrong. In your prayers try to get beyond a wicked nation or a broken marriage and identify other kinds of broken relationships: in a family, among friends, between races or nations or tribes. Then, like Hosea, focus on a broken relationship, past or present, in your own experience and in your prayers allow your mind to move from your own experience to that of others.

First, pray not for those who are in contention but for those who are caught in the crossfire.

Secondly, set down on paper the damage which the broken relationship is doing and what has been done by anyone (including the contenders) to try to put it right.

Thirdly, recalling some of the things you have read during the week, ask God to help you to come to a new view of that broken relationship so that you will be able to appreciate and respond to it differently in the future.

Finally, seek ways of helping any broken relationship that comes your way.

Now meditate on the hymn, 'Make me a channel of your peace'.

For further reading

Anthony R. Ceresko, *Introduction to the Old Testament. A Liberation Perspective*, Geoffrey Chapman, 1992

Graham I. Davies, *Hosea*, JSOT Guides, Sheffield Academic Press, 1993

Graham I. Davies, Hosea, New Century Bible Commentary, 1992

Norman K. Gottwald (ed.), *The Bible and Liberation*, Orbis, 1983

Guidelines © BRF 1997

The Bible Reading Fellowship
Peter's Way, Sandy Lane West, Oxford, OX4 5HG
ISBN 0 7459 3284 3

Distributed in Australia by:
Albatross Books Pty Ltd, PO Box 320, Sutherland,
NSW 2232

Distributed in New Zealand by:
Scripture Union Wholesale, PO Box 760, Wellington

Distributed in South Africa by:
Struik Book Distributors, PO Box 193, Maitland 7405

Distributed in the USA by:
The Bible Reading Fellowship, PO Box M, Winter
Park,
Florida 32790

Publications distributed to more than 60 countries

Cover photograph: Richard Fisher

Printed in Denmark

SUBSCRIPTIONS

NEW DAYLIGHT—GUIDELINES—LIVEWIRES

Please note our new subscription rates for 1997–1998. From **1 May 1997** the new subscription rates will be:

Individual Subscriptions covering 3 issues for under 5 copies, payable in advance (including postage and packing):

		UK	Surface	Airmail
LIVEWIRES (8–10 yr olds)	3 volumes p.a.	£12.00	£13.50	£15.00
GUIDELINES	each set of 3 p.a.	£9.30	£10.50	£12.90
NEW DAYLIGHT	each set of 3 p.a.	£9.30	£10.50	£12.90
NEW DAYLIGHT LARGE PRINT	each set of 3 p.a.	£15.00	£18.60	£21.00

Group Subscriptions covering 3 issues for 5 copies or more, sent to ONE address (post free):

LIVEWIRES	£10.50	3 volumes p.a.
GUIDELINES	£7.80	each set of 3 p.a.
NEW DAYLIGHT	£7.80	each set of 3 p.a.
NEW DAYLIGHT LARGE PRINT	£13.50	each set of 3 p.a.

Please note that the annual billing period for Group Subscriptions runs from 1 May to 30 April.

Copies of the notes may also be obtained from Christian bookshops:

LIVEWIRES	£3.50 each copy
GUIDELINES and NEW DAYLIGHT	£2.60 each copy
NEW DAYLIGHT LARGE PRINT	£4.50 each copy

Please note that the Lightning Bolts range also includes volumes of undated daily Bible reading notes for 10–14 year olds. Contact your local bookshop or BRF direct for details.

SUBSCRIPTIONS

❑ I would like to give a gift subscription (please complete both name and address sections below)
❑ I would like to take out a subscription myself (complete name and address details only once)
❑ Please send me details of Life Membership Subscriptions

This completed coupon should be sent with appropriate payment to BRF. Alternatively, please write to us quoting your name, address, the subscription you would like for either yourself or a friend (with their name and address), the start date and credit card number, expiry date and signature if paying by credit card.

Gift subscription name _____

Gift subscription address _____

_____ Postcode _____

Please send to the above, beginning with the May 1997 issue:

(please tick box)	UK	SURFACE	AIR MAIL
LIVEWIRES	❑ £12.00	❑ £13.50	❑ £15.00
GUIDELINES	❑ £9.30	❑ £10.50	❑ £12.90
NEW DAYLIGHT	❑ £9.30	❑ £10.50	❑ £12.90
NEW DAYLIGHT LARGE PRINT	❑ £15.00	❑ £18.60	❑ £21.00

Please complete the payment details below and send your coupon, with appropriate payment to: **The Bible Reading Fellowship, Peter's Way, Sandy Lane West, Oxford OX4 5HG**

Your name _____

Your address _____

_____ Postcode _____

Total enclosed £ _____ (cheques should be made payable to 'BRF')

Payment by cheque ❑ postal order ❑ Visa ❑ Mastercard ❑ Switch ❑

Card number: ☐☐☐☐ ☐☐☐☐ ☐☐☐☐ ☐☐☐☐

Expiry date of card: ☐☐☐☐   Issue number (Switch): ☐☐☐

Signature (essential if paying by credit/Switch card) _____

NB: BRF notes are also available from your local Christian bookshop.

GL0197   The Bible Reading Fellowship is a Registered Charity

BIBLE READING RESOURCES PACK

A pack of resources and ideas to help to promote Bible reading in your church is available from BRF. The pack which will be of use at any time during the year includes sample editions of the notes, magazine articles, leaflets about BRF Bible reading resources and much more. Unless you specify the month in which you would like the pack sent, we will send it immediately on receipt of your order. We greatly appreciate your donations towards the cost of producing the pack (without them we would not be able to make the pack available) and we welcome your comments about the contents of the pack and your ideas for future ones.

This coupon should be sent to:

The Bible Reading Fellowship
Peter's Way
Sandy Lane West
Oxford OX4 5HG

Name _____

Address _____

_____

_____ Postcode _____

Please send me _____ Bible Reading Resources Pack(s)

Please send the pack now/ in_____ (month).

I enclose a donation for £_____ towards the cost of the pack.

BRF PUBLICATIONS ORDER FORM

Please ensure that you complete and send off both sides of this order form.
Please send me the following book(s):

		Quantity	Price	Total
2975	Day by Day with the Psalms (*D. Cleverley Ford*)	_____	£5.99	_____
3286	Ultimate Holiday Club Guide (*A. Charter/J. Hardwick*)	_____	£9.99	_____
2985	Ultimate Holday Club Cassette (*A. Charter/J. Hardwick*) (incl VAT)	_____	£5.99	_____
3295	Livewires: Footsteps and Fingerprints (*Sharples*)	_____	£3.50	_____
3296	Livewires: Families and Feelings (*Butler*)	_____	£3.50	_____
3509	The Jesus Prayer (*S. Barrington-Ward*)	_____	£3.50	_____
3298	Searching for Truth (*J. Polkinghorne*)	_____	£6.99	_____
3539	The Apple of His Eye (*B. Plass*)	_____	£5.99	_____
3253	The Matthew Passion (*J. Fenton*)	_____	£5.99	_____
2989	What's In A Word? (book) (*D. Winter*)	_____	£5.99	_____
3072	What's In A Word? (pack) (*D. Winter*) (incl VAT)	_____	£9.99	_____
2821	People's Bible Commentary: Genesis (*H. Wansbrough*)	_____	£6.99	_____
2823	People's Bible Commentary: Hosea–Micah (*J. Tetley*)	_____	£6.99	_____
2824	People's Bible Commentary: Mark (*R.T. France*)	_____	£9.99	_____
3281	People's Bible Commentary: Galatians (*J. Fenton*)	_____	£6.99	_____
2531	Sowers and Reapers (*ed. J. Parr*)	_____	£9.99	_____
2599	Prophets and Poets (*ed. G. Emmerson*)	_____	£8.99	_____

Total cost of books £ _____

Postage and packing (see over) £ _____

TOTAL £ _____

See over for payment details. All prices are correct at time of going to press, are subject to the prevailing rate of VAT and may be subject to change without prior warning.
NB: All BRF titles are also available from your local Christian bookshop.
GL0197   The Bible Reading Fellowship is a Registered Charity

PAYMENT DETAILS

Please complete the payment details below and send with appropriate payment and completed order form to:

The Bible Reading Fellowship,
Peter's Way,
Sandy Lane West,
Oxford OX4 5HG

Name _____

Address _____

_____

_____ Postcode _____

Total enclosed £ _____ (cheques should be made payable to 'BRF')

Payment by cheque ❑ postal order ❑ Visa ❑ Mastercard ❑ Switch ❑

Card number: ☐☐☐☐ ☐☐☐☐ ☐☐☐☐ ☐☐☐☐

Expiry date of card: ☐☐☐☐   Issue number (Switch): ☐☐☐☐

Signature (essential if paying by credit/Switch card) _____

POSTAGE AND PACKING CHARGES				
order value	UK	Europe	Surface	Air Mail
£6.00 & under	£1.25	£2.25	£2.25	£3.50
£6.01–£14.99	£3.00	£3.50	£4.50	£6.50
£15.00–£29.99	£4.00	£5.50	£7.50	£11.00
£30.00 & over	free	prices on request		

Alternatively you may wish to order books using the BRF telephone order hotline:
01865 748227